Workshop on Building Linguistically Generalizable NLP Systems 2017

Copenhagen, Denmark
8 September 2017

ISBN: 978-1-5108-4747-7

Printed from e-media with permission by:

Curran Associates, Inc.
57 Morehouse Lane
Red Hook, NY 12571

Some format issues inherent in the e-media version may also appear in this print version.

Printed by Curran Associates, Inc. (2017)

Association for Computational Linguistics
209 N. Eighth Street
Stroudsburg, Pennsylvania 18360

Phone: 1-570-476-8006
Fax: 1-570-476-0860

acl@aclweb.org

Additional copies of this publication are available from:

Curran Associates, Inc.
57 Morehouse Lane
Red Hook, NY 12571 USA
Phone: 845-758-0400
Fax: 845-758-2633
Email: curran@proceedings.com
Web: www.proceedings.com

EMNLP 2017

Workshop on Building Linguistically Generalizable NLP Systems

Proceedings of the Workshop

September 8, 2017
Copenhagen, Denmark

Introduction

While the field of natural language processing has made tremendous strides as a result of machine learning techniques, systems trained within this traditional model typically do not generalize well beyond the characteristics of their training data. Especially with the influx of deep learning approaches in NLP, it is increasingly the case not only that systems are restricted in the conditions under which they work well—but also that we have little idea what exactly those conditions are.

We believe that linguistic knowledge will be instrumental to addressing these issues, so for this workshop we designed a special shared task, with the goal of bringing together researchers from NLP and linguistics to test the true linguistic generalization capacities of NLP systems. In addition to the shared task, the workshop also welcomed research contribution papers on the topic of linguistically generalizable NLP systems.

EMNLP 2017 hosts the first iteration of the Workshop on Building Linguistically Generalizable NLP Systems, in Copenhagen, Denmark on September 8, 2017.

This volume contains an overview paper describing the workshop and shared task, in addition to Shared Task Description papers from our task participants, and several Research Contribution papers. We received 13 paper submissions, including 9 in the Research Contribution track and 4 Shared Task Description track. We accepted 9 submissions: 5 Research Contributions, and 4 Shared Task Descriptions.

We are grateful to our program committee, our participants, and all authors who submitted papers for consideration, for making possible the first iteration of this workshop and shared task. We also thank the EMNLP 2017 organizers for their support.

The BLGNLP Organizers,
Emily M. Bender, Hal Daumé III, Allyson Ettinger, Sudha Rao

Organizers:

Emily M. Bender, University of Washington
Hal Daumé III, University of Maryland
Allyson Ettinger, University of Maryland
Sudha Rao, University of Maryland

Program Committee:

Doug Arnold, University of Essex
Ash Asudeh, Oxford University, Carleton University
Johan Bos, University of Groningen
Miriam Butt, Universität Konstanz
Rui Chaves, University at Buffalo
Berthold Crysmann, CNRS
Michael Yoshitaka Erlewine, National University of Singapore
Anette Frank, University of Heidelberg
Petter Haugereid, University of Bergen
Lars Hellan, Norwegian University of Science and Technology
Fabiola Henri, University of Kentucky
Julia Hockenmaier, University of Illinois at Urbana-Champaign
Jeremy G Kahn, University of Washington
Chris Kennedy, University of Chicago
Tracy King, A9
Jean-Pierre Koenig, University at Buffalo
Alex Lascarides, University of Edinburgh
Tal Linzen, Johns Hopkins University
Rob Malouf, San Diego State University
Marie-Catherine de Marneffe, The Ohio State University
Yusuke Miyao, National Institute of Informatics
Stefan Müller, Humboldt University Berlin
Tsuneko Nakazawa, University of Tokyo
Gertjan van Noord, University of Groningen
Stephan Oepen, University of Oslo
Petya Osenova, IICT-BAS
Alexis Palmer, University of North Texas
Christopher Potts, Stanford University
Matthew Purver, Queen Mary University of London
Philip Resnik, University of Maryland
Sanghoun Song, Incheon National University
Anders Søgaard, University of Copenhagen
Ida Toivonen, Carleton University
Aline Villavicencio, Federal University of Rio Grande do Sul
Tom Wasow, Stanford University
Shuly Wintner, University of Haifa
Fei Xia, University of Washington
Ping Xue, Boeing Research & Technology
Erhard Hinrichs, University of Tubingen

Invited Speakers:

Aurelie Herbelot, Universitat Pompeu Fabra
Grzegorz Chrupała, Tilburg University
Martha Palmer, University of Colorado at Boulder

Table of Contents

Conference Program

Friday, September 8, 2017

09:00–09:15 ***Welcome Note***

Towards Linguistically Generalizable NLP Systems: A Workshop and Shared Task
Allyson Ettinger, Sudha Rao, Hal Daumé III and Emily M. Bender

09:15–10:00 *Invited Talk*
Aurelie Herbelot

10:00–12:10 **Session 1: Research Contribution Papers**

10:00–10:25 *Analysing Errors of Open Information Extraction Systems*
Rudolf Schneider, Tom Oberhauser, Tobias Klatt, Felix A. Gers and Alexander Löser

10:30–11:00 ***Coffee Break***

11:00–11:45 *Invited Talk*
Grzegorz Chrupała

11:45–12:10 *Massively Multilingual Neural Grapheme-to-Phoneme Conversion*
Ben Peters, Jon Dehdari and Josef van Genabith

12:10–12:30 ***"Build It Break It, Language Edition" Shared Task Overview***

12:30–14:00 ***Lunch Break***

14:00–14:45 *Invited Talk*
Martha Palmer

Friday, September 8, 2017 (continued)

14:45–15:35 Session 2: Shared Task Description Papers

14:45–15:10 *BIBI System Description: Building with CNNs and Breaking with Deep Reinforcement Learning*
Yitong Li, Trevor Cohn and Timothy Baldwin

15:10–15:35 *Breaking NLP: Using Morphosyntax, Semantics, Pragmatics and World Knowledge to Fool Sentiment Analysis Systems*
Taylor Mahler, Willy Cheung, Micha Elsner, David King, Marie-Catherine de Marneffe, Cory Shain, Symon Stevens-Guille and Michael White

15:35–16:00 *Coffee Break*

16:00–17:15 Poster Session

An Adaptable Lexical Simplification Architecture for Major Ibero-Romance Languages
Daniel Ferrés, Horacio Saggion and Xavier Gómez Guinovart

Cross-genre Document Retrieval: Matching between Conversational and Formal Writings
Tomasz Jurczyk and Jinho D. Choi

ACTSA: Annotated Corpus for Telugu Sentiment Analysis
Sandeep Sricharan Mukku and Radhika Mamidi

Strawman: An Ensemble of Deep Bag-of-Ngrams for Sentiment Analysis
Kyunghyun Cho

Breaking Sentiment Analysis of Movie Reviews
Ieva Staliūnaitė and Ben Bonfil

17:15–17:30 *Closing Remarks*

Towards Linguistically Generalizable NLP Systems: A Workshop and Shared Task

Allyson Ettinger[△♡] **Sudha Rao**[♣♡] **Hal Daumé III**[△♣◇♡▽] **Emily M. Bender**[♠]
University of Maryland: Linguistics[△], Computer Science[♣], Language Science[◇] and UMIACS[♡]
University of Washington Department of Linguistics[♠]
Microsoft Research New York[▽]
{aetting@, raosudha@cs., hal@umiacs.}umd.edu, ebender@uw.edu

Abstract

This paper presents a summary of the first Workshop on Building Linguistically Generalizable Natural Language Processing Systems, and the associated *Build It Break It, The Language Edition* shared task. The goal of this workshop was to bring together researchers in NLP and linguistics with a shared task aimed at testing the generalizability of NLP systems beyond the distributions of their training data. We describe the motivation, setup, and participation of the shared task, provide discussion of some highlighted results, and discuss lessons learned.

1 Introduction

Machine learning techniques have had tremendously positive impact on the field of natural language processing, to the point that we now have systems for many NLP problems that work extremely well—at least when the NLP problem is carefully designed and these systems are tested on data that looks like their training data. Especially with the influx of deep learning approaches to NLP, we find ourselves more and more in the situation that we have systems that work well under some conditions, but we (and the models!) may have little idea what those conditions are.

We believe that linguistic knowledge is critical in many phases of the NLP pipeline, including:

1. Task design and choice of language(s)
2. Annotation schema design
3. System architecture design and/or feature design
4. Evaluation design and error analysis
5. Generalization beyond training data

Our goal in this workshop was to bring together researchers from NLP and linguistics through a carefully designed shared task. This shared task was designed to test the true generalization ability of NLP systems beyond the distribution of data on which they may have been trained. In addition to the shared task, the workshop also welcomed research contribution papers.

In this paper, we describe the shared task, laying out our motivations for pursuing this twist on the traditional set up (§2) and the various design decisions we made as we took the initial idea and worked to shape it into something that would be feasible for participants and informative for our field (§3). We then go on to describe our data (§4), the participating systems and breaker approaches (§5), and our approach to scoring (§6). Finally, we give an overview of the shared task results in §7, and discuss lessons learned in §8.

Our hope is that in laying out the successes and challenges of the first iteration of this shared task, we can help future shared tasks of this type to build on our experience. To this end, we also make available the datasets collected for and created during the shared task (§4).

2 Motivation: Robust NLP Systems

Natural language processing has largely embraced the "independently and identically distributed" (iid) probably-approximately-correct (PAC) model of learning from the machine learning community (c.f. Valiant, 1984), typically under a uniform cost function. This model has been so successful that it often simply goes unquestioned as the "right way" to do NLP. Under this model, any phenomenon that is sufficiently rare in a given corpus (seen as a "distribution of data") is not worth addressing. Systems are not typically built to handle tail phenomena, and iid-based learning

Proceedings of the First Workshop on Building Linguistically Generalizable NLP Systems, pages 1–10
Copenhagen, Denmark, September 8, 2017.

similarly trains systems to ignore such phenomena. This problem is exacerbated by frequent use of overly simplistic loss functions, which further encourage systems to ignore phenomena that they do not capture adequately.

The result is that NLP systems are quite brittle in the face of infrequent linguistic phenomena,[1] a characteristic which stands in stark contrast to human language users, who at a very young age can make subtle distinctions that have little support in the distribution of data they've been exposed to (c.f., Legate and Yang, 2002; Crain and Nakayama, 1987). This ability also allows humans to avoid making certain errors due to over- or under-exposure. A computational counter-example is ignoring negations because they are relatively infrequent and typically only have a small effect on the loss function used in training.

The brittleness of current NLP systems, and the substantial discrepancy between their capacities and that of humans, suggests that there is much left to be desired in the traditional "iid" model. This applies not only to training and testing, but also to error analysis: iid development data is unlikely to exhibit all the linguistic phenomena that we might be interested in testing. Even if one is uninterested in the scientific questions addressed by testing a model's ability to handle less frequent phenomena, it should be noted that any NLP system that is released is likely to be adversarially tested by users who want to break it for fun.

This state of affairs has not gone unnoticed. On the one hand, there is work on creating targeted evaluation datasets that exhibit and are annotated for particular linguistic phenomena, in order to facilitate fine-grained analysis of the linguistic capacities of systems for tasks such as parsing, entailment, and semantic relatedness (Rimell et al., 2009; Bender et al., 2011; Marelli et al., 2014). Additionally, there is an increasing amount of work on developing methods of exposing exactly what linguistic knowledge NLP models develop (Kádár et al., 2016; Li et al., 2015) and what linguistic information is encoded in models' produced representations (Adi et al., 2016; Ettinger et al., 2016). Our aim in organizing this workshop was to build on this foundation, designing the shared task to generate data specifically created to identify the boundaries of systems' linguistic capacities, and welcoming further related research contributions to stimulate additional discussion.

3 Shared Task: *Build It Break It, The Language Edition*

To address the issues identified above, we developed a shared task inspired by the Build It Break It Fix It Contest[2] and adapted for application to NLP. The shared task proceeded in three phases: a building phase, a breaking phase, and a scoring phase:

1. In the first phase, "builders" take a designated NLP task and develop techniques to solve it.

2. In the second phase, "breakers", having seen the output of the builders' systems on some development data, are tasked with constructing minimal-pair test cases intended to identify the boundaries of the systems' capabilities.

3. In the third phase, builders run their systems on the newly created minimal pair test set and provide their predictions for scoring.

Builders are scored based how well their systems can withstand the attacks of breakers, and breakers are scored based on how well they can identify system boundaries.

The goals of this type of shared task are multifold: we want to build more reliable NLP technology, by stress-testing against an adversary; we want to learn more about what linguistic phenomena our systems are capable of handling so that we can guide research in interesting directions; we want to encourage researchers to think about what assumptions their models are implicitly making by asking them to break them; we want to engage linguists in the process of testing NLP systems; we want to build a test collection of examples that are not necessarily high probability under the distribution of the training data, but are nonetheless representative of language phenomena that we expect a reasonable NLP system to handle; and we want to increase cross-talk between linguistics and natural language processing researchers.

[1]During a panel at the 1st Workshop on Representation Learning for NLP (ACL 2016; `https://sites.google.com/site/repl4nlp2016/`) some panelists acknowledged the fact that they could probably break any NLP system with very little effort—meaning it shouldn't be hard to invent reasonable examples that would confuse the systems.

[2]`https://builditbreakit.org`

Sentence	UCD finished the 2006 championship as Dublin champions, by beating St Vincents in the final.
Predicate	beating
Question	Who beat someone?
Answer	UCD

Figure 1: Example QA-SRL item

3.1 Task Selection

In selecting the NLP task to be solved by the builders, we had a number of considerations. The task should be one that requires strong linguistic capabilities, so that in identifying the boundaries of the systems, breakers are encouraged to target linguistic phenomena key to increasing the robustness of language understanding. Additionally, we want the task to be without significant barrier to entry, to encourage builder participation.

In the interest of balancing these considerations and testing the effectiveness of different tasks, we ran two tasks in parallel: sentiment analysis and question-answer driven semantic role labeling (QA-SRL; He et al., 2015). The sentiment task consists of standard sentiment analysis performed on movie reviews. In the QA-SRL task, the input is a sentence and a question related to one of the predicates in the sentence, and the output is a span of the sentence that answers the question. See Figure 1 for an example item. The task allows for testing semantic role labeling without the need for a pre-defined set of roles, or for annotators with significant training or linguistic expertise.

3.2 Building

From the builders' point of view, the shared task is similar to other typical shared tasks in our field. Task organizers provide training and development data, and the builder teams create systems on the basis of that data. We do not distinguish open versus closed tracks (use of provided training data is optional). Our goal was to attract a variety of approaches, both knowledge engineering-based and machine learning-based.

We considered requiring builders to submit system code as an alternative to running their systems on two different datasets (see Section 4). However, ultimately we decided in favor of builder teams running their own systems and submitting predictions in both phases.

3.3 Breaking

The task of breaker teams was to construct minimal pairs to be used as test input to the builder systems, with the goal of identifying the boundaries of system capacities. In order for a test pair to be effective in identifying a system's boundaries, it needs to satisfy two requirements:

1. The system succeeds on one item of the pair but fails on the other.

2. The difference between the items in the pair is specific enough that the ability of the system to handle one but not the other can be attributed to an identifiable cause.

Satisfaction of requirement 1 is what we will refer to as "breaking" a system (note that this also applies if the system fails on the original example but succeeds on the hand-constructed variant).

Breakers were thus instructed to create minimal pairs on which they expected systems to make a correct prediction on one but not the other of the items. Breakers were additionally asked, while constructing minimal pairs, to keep in mind what exactly they would be able to conclude about a system's linguistic capacity if it proved able to handle one item of a given pair but not the other. Along this line, breakers were encouraged to provide a rationale with each minimal pair, to explain their reasoning in making a given change.[3]

In order to exert a certain amount of control over the domain and style of breakers' items, we required breakers to work from data provided for each task. Specifically, we asked them to select sentences from the provided dataset and make targeted changes in order to create their minimal pairs. This means that each minimal pair consisted of one unaltered sentence from the original dataset and one sentence reflecting the breakers' change to that sentence. This was done to ensure that systems had at least a reasonable chance at success, by scoping down the range of possible variants that breakers could provide.

As an example, let us say that the provided sentiment analysis dataset includes the sentence *I love this movie*, which has positive sentiment (+1). A breaker team could then construct a pair such as the following:

(1) +1 I love this movie!

[3]Breaker instructions can be found here: `https://bibinlp.umiacs.umd.edu/sharedtask.html`

+1 I'm mad for this movie!

While the first item is likely straightforward to classify, we might anticipate a simple sentiment system to fail on the second, since it may flag the word *mad* as indicating negative sentiment. Breakers could choose to change the sentiment with their modification, or let it remain the same.

For the QA-SRL task, breakers were only to change the original sentence (and, if appropriate, the answer), leaving the question unaltered. For instance, breakers could generate the following item to be paired with the example in Figure 1:

(2) **Sent′** UCD finished the 2006 championship as Dublin champions, when they beat St Vincents in the final.
Ans′ UCD (unchanged)

We might anticipate that the system would now predict the pronoun *they* as the answer to the question, without resolving to UCD.[4]

The sets of minimal pairs created by the breakers then constituted the test set of the shared task, which was sent to builders to generate predictions on for scoring.

4 Shared Task Data

4.1 Training Data

For the sentiment training data, we used the Sentiment Treebank dataset from Socher et al. (2013), developed from the Rotten Tomatoes review dataset of Pang and Lee (2005).[5] Each sentence in the dataset has a sentiment value between 0 and 1, as well as sentiment values for the phrases in its syntactic parse. In order to establish a binary labeling scheme at the sentence level, we mapped sentences in range (0, 0.4) to "negative" and sentences in range (0.6, 1.0) to "positive". Neutral sentences—those with a sentiment value between 0.4 and 0.6—were removed. The sentiment training data had a total of 6921 sentences and 166738 phrases. Phrase-level sentiment labels were made available to participants as an optional resource.

For QA-SRL training data, we used the data created by He et al. (2015).[6] These items were drawn from Wikipedia, and each item of the training data includes the sentence (with the relevant predicate identified), the question, and the answer. The training data had a total of 5149 sentences.

4.2 Blind Development Data

Blind dev data was provided for builders to submit initial predictions on, as produced by their systems. These predictions were made available for breakers, to be used as a reference when creating test minimal pairs. For sentiment, we collected an additional 500 sentences from a pool of Rotten Tomatoes reviews for movies in the years 2003-2005. For annotations, we used the same method of annotation via crowd-sourcing that was used by Socher et al. (2013). For QA-SRL, we extracted a set of 814 sentences from Wikipedia and annotated these by crowd-sourcing, following the method of He et al. (2015).

4.3 Starter Data for Breakers

As described above, breakers were given data from which to draw items that could then be altered to create minimal pairs. Sentiment breakers were provided an additional set of 500 sentiment sentences, collected and annotated by the same method as that used for the 500 blind dev sentences for sentiment. QA-SRL breakers were provided an additional set of 814 items, collected and annotated by the same method as the blind dev items for QA-SRL.

4.4 Test Data

The test data for evaluating builder systems consisted of the minimal pairs constructed by the breaker teams. The labels for the pairs were provided by the breakers themselves, though additional crowd-sourced labels were made available for teams to check for any substantial deviations.

We release the minimal pair test sets, as well as annotated blind dev and starter data for sentiment and QA-SRL: `https://bibinlp.umiacs.umd.edu/data`.

[4] Breakers were not allowed to change the sentence such that the accompanying question was no longer answerable with a substring from the original sentence. For instance, breakers could not make a change such as *Terry fed Parker* → *Parker was fed* with an accompanying test question of *Who fed Parker?*, since the answer to that question would no longer be contained in the sentence.

[5] Sentiment training data available here: `https://nlp.stanford.edu/sentiment/`

[6] QA-SRL training data available here: `https://dada.cs.washington.edu/qasrl/`.

5 Task Participants

5.1 Builder Teams: Sentiment

Strawman Kyunghyun Cho contributed a sentiment analysis system intended to serve as a naïve baseline for the shared task. This model, called Strawman, consisted of an ensemble of five deep bag-of-ngrams multilayer perceptron classifiers. The model's vocabulary was composed of the most frequent 100k n-grams from the provided training data, with n up to 2 (Cho, 2017).

University of Melbourne, CNNs The builder team from University of Melbourne (which also participated as a breaker team), contributed two sentiment analysis systems consisting of convolutional neural networks. One CNN was trained on data labeled at the phrase level (PCNN), and the other was trained on data labeled at the sentence level (SCNN) (Li et al., 2017).

Recursive Neural Tensor Network To supplement our submitted builder systems, we tested several additional sentiment analysis systems on the breaker test set. The first of these was the Stanford Recursive Neural Tensor Network (RNTN) (Socher et al., 2013). This model is a recursive neural network-based sentiment classifier, composing words and phrases of input sentences based on binary branching syntactic structure, and using the composed representations as input features to softmax classifiers at every syntactic node. This model, rather than parameterizing the composition function by the words being composed (Socher et al., 2012), uses a single more powerful tensor-based composition function for composing each node of the syntactic tree.

DCNN The second supplementary sentiment system was the Dynamic Convolutional Neural Network from University of Oxford (Kalchbrenner et al., 2014). This is a convolutional neural network sentiment classifier that uses interleaved one-dimensional convolutional layers and dynamic k-max pooling layers, and handles input sequences of varying length.

Bag-of-ngram features Finally, we tested an additional bag-of-ngrams sentiment system with n up to 3, consisting of a linear classifier, implemented by one of the organizers in vowpal wabbit (Langford et al., 2007).

5.2 Breaker Teams: Sentiment

Utrecht The breaker team from Utrecht University used a variety of strategies, including insertion of modals and opinion adverbs that convey speaker stance, changes based in world knowledge, and pragmatic and syntactic changes (Staliūnaitė and Bonfil, 2017).

Ohio State University The breaker team from OSU also used a variety of strategies, classified as morphosyntactic, semantic, pragmatic, and world knowledge-based changes, to target hypothesized weaknesses in the sentiment analysis systems (Mahler et al., 2017).

University of Melbourne The breaker team from University of Melbourne opted to generate test minimal pairs automatically, borrowing from methods for generating adversarial examples in computer vision. They used reinforcement learning, optimizing on reversed labels, to identify tokens or phrases to be changed, and then applied a substitution method (Li et al., 2017). Some human supervision was used to ensure grammaticality and correct labeling of the sentences.

Team 4 The fourth sentiment breaker team did not submit a description paper, but the results from this team's test set are reported below.

5.3 Builder Team: QA-SRL

The organizers provided a QA-SRL system, as there were no external builder submissions for this task. The provided system was a logistic regression classifier, trained with 1-through-5 skip-grams with a maximum skip of 4. Potential answers were neighbors and neighbors-of-neighbors in a dependency parse of the sentence (Stanford dependency parser; De Marneffe et al., 2006), and input to the classifier was the predicate, question verb, question string, and dependency relation between the predicate and the potential answer. An answer was marked as correct at training time if it overlapped at least 75% in characters with the true answer.

5.4 Breaker Team: QA-SRL

There was one breaker submission for QA-SRL. This team did not submit a description paper—however, the rationales provided for their submitted minimal pairs indicate that they made a variety of changes including adding modifiers, adding or changing prepositional phrases, substituting synonyms, using distractor noun phrases, and targeting pronoun resolution.

6 Shared Task Scoring

For the purpose of scoring, a test minimal pair is considered to have "broken" a system if one item of the pair gets a correct prediction and the other item gets an incorrect prediction. As outlined above, this is to reward breakers for zeroing in on system boundaries.

For scoring the breakers, we decided to use the average across systems of the product of the system dev set accuracy and system breaking percentage. Specifically, if a breaker j provides a set of examples D_j to break systems $i = 1 \ldots N$, then the breaker score is:

$$\text{score}(j) = \frac{1}{N}\sum_{i=1}^{N} \text{acc}_i(\text{dev})\frac{\text{break}(i,j)}{|D_j|} \quad (1)$$

$$\text{acc}_i(\text{dev}) = \text{accuracy of system } i \text{ on dev} \quad (2)$$

$$\text{break}(i,j) = \#x \in D_j \text{ that break system } i \quad (3)$$

The motivation here is to weight breaker successes against a given system by the general strength of that system.

For scoring the builders, we used two metrics:

1. Average F score across all sentences (originals and modified) for all breaker teams
2. Percentage of sentence pairs that break system.

7 Results and Discussion

Since our participation in the QA-SRL task was minimal, we focus in this section on the results for the sentiment analysis task.

7.1 Aggregate Results

Aggregate results for builders are shown in Table 1. Computing by F1 score, Strawman comes out on top among builder systems with an average F1 of 0.528, followed by the phrase-based CNN and bag-of-ngrams. When scored by percentage of pairs that break the system, the phrase-based CNN comes out on top, broken by 24.39% of test pairs. The bag-of-ngrams model and DCNN follow closely behind, while the sentence-based CNN falls last by a fair margin.

Aggregate results for breakers are shown in Table 2. By our chosen scoring metric, the team from

System	average F1	% broken test cases
Strawman	**0.528**	25.43
Phrase-based CNN	0.518	**24.39**
Bag-of-ngrams	0.510	24.74
Sentence-based CNN	0.490	28.57
DCNN	0.483	25.09
RNTN	0.457	25.96

Table 1: Builder team scores: Average F1 across all breaker test cases, and percent of breaker test cases that broke the system

Breaker	score
Utrecht	**31.17**
OSU	28.66
Melbourne	19.28
Team 4	7.48

Table 2: Breaker team scores

Utrecht falls in first place among breaker teams, followed closely by the breaker team from OSU.

7.2 Detailed Results

Aggregate scores obscure the important details that we aim to probe for with this shared task, namely the particular weaknesses of a given system targeted by a given minimal pair or set of minimal pairs. Figure 2 brings us closer to the desired granularity with individual breaking percentages, allowing us a clearer sense of the interaction between breaker team and builder system.

Some patterns emerge. The Utrecht and OSU breaker team are roughly on par across systems, with Utrecht pulling ahead by the largest margin on Strawman. These teams seem to have used a comparable variety of linguistically diverse and targeted attacks, which may explain the fact that they perform similarly.

The Melbourne test set stood out from the others in that it was automatically generated. As might be expected, this test set lags behind in breaking percentage against most systems—however, against the sentence-based CNN it performs on par with the other two teams.

The Team 4 test set has the lowest overall breaking percentages by a substantial margin. One interesting note is that this team's test set receives one of its lowest breaking percentages against the

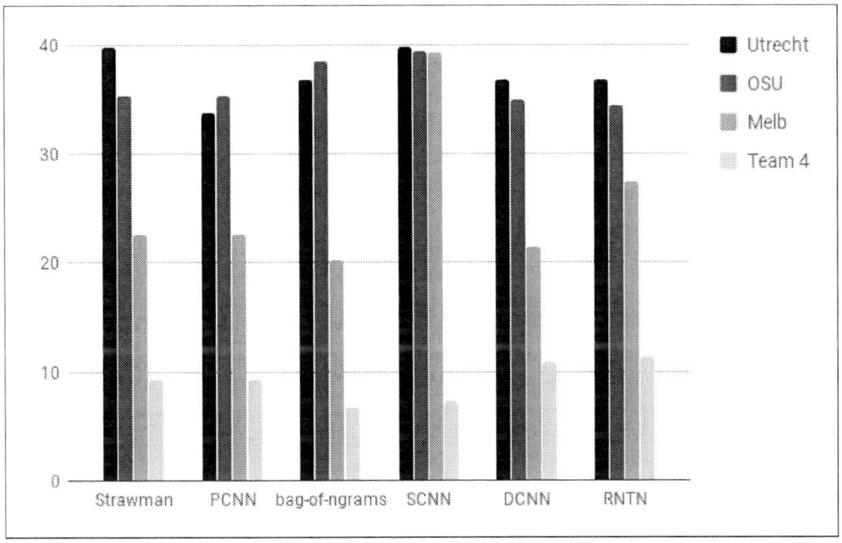

Figure 2: Detailed breaking percentages

sentence-based CNN, which was the source of some of the highest breaking percentages for the other breaker teams.

7.3 Item-based Results

It is of course at the level of individual minimal pairs that our analysis of this shared task can have the most power. Tables 3 and 4 show a sample of breaker minimal pairs and builder system predictions on those pairs, allowing us to observe system performance at the item level for this sample. These examples were chosen with the goal of finding interesting strategies that break some systems but not others, in order to explore differences. However, we found that for a majority of successful test pairs, systems tended to break together.

On Utrecht pair 1a/b, we see that the addition of the word *pain* breaks Strawman and bag-of-ngrams, as we might expect from ngram-based systems. Apart from RNTN, which makes incorrect predictions on both items, the remaining systems are able to handle this change.

On Utrecht pair 2a/b, we see that bag-of-ngrams, DCNN, SCNN and RNTN all break, though in different directions, with SCNN and RNTN getting the altered sentence wrong, and bag-of-ngrams and DCNN getting the original sentence wrong. This suggests a lack of sensitivity to the subtly different sentiments conveyed in context by the substituted words *unnerving* and *hilarious*. Strawman and PCNN, however, predict both items correctly.

The substitution of the comparative phrase in OSU pair 1a/b impressively breaks every system, suggesting that the sentiment conveyed by the phrase *just willing enough* in context is beyond the capacity of any of the systems. The sarcasm addition in OSU 2a/b breaks Strawman, bag-of-ngrams and DCNN, but not SCNN or RNTN (while PCNN breaks in the opposite direction).

Strawman breaks on Melbourne 1a/b, which is interesting as we might expect the substituted item *thrill* to be flagged as carrying positive sentiment. Bag-of-ngrams fails on both items of the pair, and RNTN gives a neutral label for the second item.

Melbourne 2a/b employs a word re-ordering technique and breaks every system in various directions—except for bag-of-ngrams and RNTN, which fail on both items—suggesting that both the original and altered sentences of this pair give systems trouble.

Team 4 1a/b fools bag-of-ngrams with the altered sentence, while DCNN and RNTN make incorrect predictions on the original.

As we can see in these examples, by testing systems on minimal pair test items such as these we have the potential to zero in on the linguistic phenomena that any given system can and cannot handle. It is also clear that it is specifically when a system "breaks" (makes a correct prediction on one but not the other item), and when the change in the pair is targeted enough, that we are able to draw straightforward conclusions. For instance, OSU pair 1a/b allows us to conclude that inferring the positive effect of the phrase *just [...] enough* on a previously negative context is beyond the systems' capacities. On the other hand, the more diffuse changes in Melbourne pair 2a/b make it more difficult to determine the precise cause of a system breaking in one direction or the other.

Of course, to be more confident about our conclusions, we would want to analyze system predictions on multiple different pairs that target the same linguistic phenomenon. This can be a goal for future iterations and analyses.

8 Lessons for the Future

A variety of lessons came out of the shared task, which can be helpful for future iterations or future shared tasks of this type. We describe some of these lessons here.

The choice of NLP task is an important one. While QA-SRL is a promising task in terms of requiring linguistic robustness, it yielded lower participation than sentiment analysis. Strategies for encouraging buy-in from both builders and breakers will be important. One strategy would be to team up with existing shared tasks, to which we could add a breaking phase.

While going through the labels assigned to the minimal pairs by breaker teams, we find some label choices to be questionable. Since unreliable labels will skew the assessment of builder performance, in future iterations there should be an additional phase in which we validate breaker labels with an external source (e.g., crowd-sourcing). To minimize cost and time, this could be done only for examples that are "contested" by either builders or other breakers.

The notion of a "minimal pair" is critical to this task, so it is important that we define the notion clearly, and that we ensure that submitted pairs conform to this definition. Reviewing breaker submissions, we find that in some cases breakers have significantly changed the sentence, in ways that may not conform to our original expectations. In future iterations, it will be important to have clear and concrete definitions of minimal pair, and it would also be useful to have some external review of the pairs to confirm that they are permissible.

For this year's shared task we chose to limit breakers by requiring them to draw from existing data for creating their pairs. A potential variation to consider would be allowing breaker teams to create their own sentence pairs from scratch, in addition to drawing from existing sentences (with the restriction that sentences should fall in the specified domain). This greater freedom for breakers may increase the range of linguistic phenomena able to be targeted, and the precision with which breakers can target them.

Finally, it is important to consider general strategies for encouraging participation. We identify two potential areas for improvement. First, the timeline of this year's shared task was shorter than would be optimal, which placed an undue burden in particular on builders, who needed to run systems and submit predictions in two different phases. A longer timeline could make participation more feasible. Second, participants may be reluctant to submit work to be broken—to address this, we might consider anonymous system submissions in the future.

9 Conclusion

The First Workshop on Building Linguistically Generalizable NLP systems, and the associated first iteration of the *Build It Break It, The Language Edition* shared task, allowed us to begin exploring the limits of current NLP systems with respect to specific linguistic phenomena, and to extract lessons to build on in future iterations or future shared tasks of this type. We have described the details and results of the shared task, and discussed lessons to be applied in the future. We are confident that tasks such as this, that emphasize testing the effectiveness of NLP systems in handling of linguistic phenomena beyond the training data distributions, can make significant contributions to improving the robustness and quality of NLP systems as a whole.

Acknowledgments

The authors would like to acknowledge Chris Dyer who, as a panelist at the Workshop on Representation Learning for NLP, made the original observation about the brittleness of NLP systems which led to the conception of the current workshop and shared task. We would also like to thank the UMD Computational Linguistics and Information Processing lab, and the UMD Language Science Center. This work was partially supported by NSF grants NRT-1449815 and IIS-1618193, and an NSF Graduate Research Fellowship to Allyson

ID	Minimal Pairs	Label	Rationale
Utrecht 1a	Through elliptical and seemingly oblique methods, he forges moments of staggering **emotional power**	+1	*Emotional pain can be positive*
Utrecht 1b	Through elliptical and seemingly oblique methods, he forges moments of staggering **emotional pain**	+1	
Utrecht 2a	[Bettis] has a smoldering, humorless intensity that's **unnerving**.	-1	*Funny can be positive & negative*
Utrecht 2b	[Bettis] has a smoldering, humorless intensity that's **hilarious**.	+1	
OSU 1a	A bizarre (and sometimes repulsive) exercise that's **a little too willing** to swoon in its own weird embrace.	-1	*Comparative*
OSU 1b	A bizarre (and sometimes repulsive) exercise that's **just willing enough** to swoon in its own weird embrace.	+1	
OSU 2a	Proves that **fresh new work** can be done in the horror genre if the director follows his or her own shadowy muse.	+1	*Sarcasm (single cue)*
OSU 2b	Proves that **dull new work** can be done in the horror genre if the director follows his or her own shadowy muse.	-1	
Melbourne 1a	Exactly the kind of **unexpected delight** one hopes for every time the lights go down.	+1	*(Not provided)*
Melbourne 1b	Exactly the kind of **thrill** one hopes for every time the lights go down.	+1	
Melbourne 2a	**American drama** doesn't get any more meaty and muscular **than this**.	+1	*(Not provided)*
Melbourne 2b	**This** doesn't get any more meaty and muscular **than American drama**.	-1	
Team4 1a	Rarely have good intentions been wrapped in such a **sticky** package.	-1	*(Not provided)*
Team4 1b	Rarely have good intentions been wrapped in such a **adventurous** package.	+1	

Table 3: **Sample minimal pairs**: Examples of minimal pairs created by different breaker teams with the minimal changes highlighted. 'Label' is the label provided to the pairs by the breaker teams.

ID	True Label	Strawman	PCNN	Bag-of-ngrams	SCNN	DCNN	RNTN
Utrecht 1a	+1	+1	+1	+1	+1	+1	-1
Utrecht 1b	+1	-1	+1	-1	+1	+1	-1
Utrecht 2a	-1	-1	-1	+1	-1	+1	-1
Utrecht 2b	+1	+1	+1	+1	-1	+1	-1
OSU 1a	-1	-1	-1	-1	-1	-1	-1
OSU 1b	+1	-1	-1	-1	-1	-1	-1
OSU 2a	+1	+1	-1	+1	+1	+1	+1
OSU 2b	-1	+1	-1	+1	-1	+1	-1
Melbourne 1a	+1	+1	+1	-1	+1	+1	+1
Melbourne 1b	+1	-1	+1	-1	+1	+1	0
Melbourne 2a	+1	-1	+1	-1	-1	-1	-1
Melbourne 2b	-1	-1	+1	+1	-1	-1	0
Team4 1a	-1	-1	-1	-1	-1	+1	+1
Team4 1b	+1	+1	+1	-1	+1	+1	+1

Table 4: **Sample minimal pair predictions**: Builder system predictions on the example minimal pairs from Table 3. 'True Label' is the label provided to the pairs by the breaker teams.

Ettinger under Grant No. DGE 1322106. Any opinions, findings, conclusions, or recommendations expressed here are those of the authors and do not necessarily reflect the view of the sponsor(s).

References

Yossi Adi, Einat Kermany, Yonatan Belinkov, Ofer Lavi, and Yoav Goldberg. 2016. Fine-grained analysis of sentence embeddings using auxiliary prediction tasks. *arXiv preprint arXiv:1608.04207*.

Emily M. Bender, Dan Flickinger, Stephan Oepen, and Yi Zhang. 2011. Parser evaluation over local and non-local deep dependencies in a large corpus. In *Proceedings of the 2011 Conference on Empirical Methods in Natural Language Processing*, pages 397–408, Edinburgh, Scotland, UK. Association for Computational Linguistics.

Kyunghyun Cho. 2017. Recursive deep models for semantic compositionality over a sentiment treebank. In *Proceedings of the Workshop on Building Linguistically Generalizable NLP Systems*.

Stephen Crain and Mineharu Nakayama. 1987. Structure dependence in grammar formation. *Language*, pages 522–543.

Marie-Catherine De Marneffe, Bill MacCartney, Christopher D Manning, et al. 2006. Generating typed dependency parses from phrase structure parses. In *Proceedings of LREC*, volume 6, pages 449–454. Genoa Italy.

Allyson Ettinger, Ahmed Elgohary, and Philip Resnik. 2016. Probing for semantic evidence of composition by means of simple classification tasks. *ACL 2016*, page 134.

Luheng He, Mike Lewis, and Luke Zettlemoyer. 2015. Question-answer driven semantic role labeling: Using natural language to annotate natural language. In *Proceedings of the Conference on Empirical Methods in Natural Language Processing*, pages 643–653.

Ákos Kádár, Grzegorz Chrupała, and Afra Alishahi. 2016. Representation of linguistic form and function in recurrent neural networks. *arXiv preprint arXiv:1602.08952*.

Nal Kalchbrenner, Edward Grefenstette, and Phil Blunsom. 2014. A convolutional neural network for modelling sentences. *arXiv preprint arXiv:1404.2188*.

J Langford, L Li, and A Strehl. 2007. Vowpal wabbit online learning project.

Julie Anne Legate and Charles D Yang. 2002. Empirical re-assessment of stimulus poverty arguments. *The Linguistic Review*, 18(1-2):151–162.

Jiwei Li, Xinlei Chen, Eduard Hovy, and Dan Jurafsky. 2015. Visualizing and understanding neural models in nlp. *arXiv preprint arXiv:1506.01066*.

Yitong Li, Trevor Cohn, and Timothy Baldwin. 2017. Bibi system description: Building with cnns and breaking with deep reinforcement learning. In *Proceedings of the Workshop on Building Linguistically Generalizable NLP Systems*.

Taylor Mahler, Willy Cheung, Micha Elsner, David King, Marie-Catherine de Marneffe, Cory Shain, Symon Stevens-Guille, and Michael White. 2017. Breaking nlp: Using morphosyntax, semantics, pragmatics and world knowledge to fool sentiment analysis systems. In *Proceedings of the Workshop on Building Linguistically Generalizable NLP Systems*.

Marco Marelli, Stefano Menini, Marco Baroni, Luisa Bentivogli, Raffaella Bernardi, and Roberto Zamparelli. 2014. A SICK cure for the evaluation of compositional distributional semantic models. In *Language Resources and Evaluation*, pages 216–223.

Bo Pang and Lillian Lee. 2005. Seeing stars: Exploiting class relationships for sentiment categorization with respect to rating scales. In *Proceedings of the 43rd Annual Meeting of the Association for Computational Linguistics*, pages 115–124. Association for Computational Linguistics.

Laura Rimell, Stephen Clark, and Mark Steedman. 2009. Unbounded dependency recovery for parser evaluation. In *Proceedings of the 2009 Conference on Empirical Methods in Natural Language Processing*, pages 813–821, Singapore. Association for Computational Linguistics.

Richard Socher, Brody Huval, Christopher D Manning, and Andrew Y Ng. 2012. Semantic compositionality through recursive matrix-vector spaces. In *Proceedings of the 2012 Joint Conference on Empirical Methods in Natural Language Processing and Computational Natural Language Learning*, pages 1201–1211. Association for Computational Linguistics.

Richard Socher, Alex Perelygin, Jean Y Wu, Jason Chuang, Christopher D Manning, Andrew Y Ng, Christopher Potts, et al. 2013. Recursive deep models for semantic compositionality over a sentiment treebank. In *Proceedings of the Conference on Empirical Methods in Natural Language Processing*, volume 1631, page 1642.

Ieva Staliūnaitė and Ben Bonfil. 2017. Breaking sentiment analysis of movie reviews. In *Proceedings of the Workshop on Building Linguistically Generalizable NLP Systems*.

Leslie G Valiant. 1984. A theory of the learnable. *Communications of the ACM*, 27(11):1134–1142.

Analysing Errors of Open Information Extraction Systems

Rudolf Schneider, Tom Oberhauser, Tobias Klatt,
Felix A. Gers and **Alexander Löser**
{rudolf.schneider, tom.oberhauser, tobias.klatt, gers, aloeser}@beuth-hochschule.de
Beuth University of Applied Sciences Berlin
Luxemburger Str. 10, 13353 Berlin, Germany

Abstract

We report results on benchmarking Open Information Extraction (OIE) systems using RelVis, a toolkit for benchmarking Open Information Extraction systems. Our comprehensive benchmark contains three data sets from the news domain and one data set from Wikipedia with overall 4522 labeled sentences and 11243 binary or n-ary OIE relations. In our analysis on these data sets we compared the performance of four popular OIE systems, ClausIE, OpenIE 4.2, Stanford OpenIE and PredPatt. In addition, we evaluated the impact of five common error classes on a subset of 749 n-ary tuples. From our deep analysis we unreveal important research directions for a next generation of OIE systems.

1 Introduction

Open Information Extraction (OIE) is an important intermediate step of the nlp stack for many text mining tasks, such as summarization, relation extraction, knowledge base construction and question answering (Mausam, 2016; Stanovsky et al., 2015; Khot et al., 2017). OIE systems are designed for extracting n-ary tuples from diverse and large amounts of text, without being restricted to a fixed schema or domain. These tuples consist of one predicate and n arguments e.g: *flew*(Obama; from Berlin; to New York).

Users often desire to select a suitable OIE system for their specific application domain. Making the right choice is not an easy task. Unfortunately, there is surprisingly little work on evaluating and comparing results among different OIE systems. Worse, most OIE methods utilize proprietary and unpublished data sets. In most cases users can only rely on publications and need to download, compile and apply existing systems to their own data sets.

Contribution Ideally, one could compare different OIE systems with a unified benchmarking suite. As a result, the user could identify "sweet spots" of each system but also weaknesses for common error classes. The benchmarking suite should feature a diverse set of gold annotations with several thousands of annotated sentences. By exploring results and errors, the user can learn how to design the next generation of OIE systems or how to combine several systems into an ensemble.

Our contributions are: (1) We report results of a quantitative analysis on four commonly used OIE systems: STANFORD OPENIE (SIE) (Angeli et al., 2015), OPENIE 4.2 (OIE)[1], CLAUSIE (CIE) (Del Corro and Gemulla, 2013) or PREDPAT (PP) (White et al., 2016). Which employ rule based as well as machine learning based methods on linguistic structures like dependency parses. These were applied on *4522* sentences and *11243* n-ary gold standard tuples. (2) We share in-depth insights on a qualitative error analysis of *749* n-ary tuples in *68* sentences from four gold standard data sets annotated by all four OIE systems. (3) We provide an integrated benchmark for OIE systems consisting of three news data sets NYT-222, WEB-500 (Mesquita et al., 2013), PENN-100 (Xu et al., 2013) and a large OIE benchmark from Newswire and Wikipedia (Stanovsky and Dagan, 2016) combined in our evaluation tool *RelVis*. Our benchmark tool will be provided to the community under an open source license.

The remainder of this paper is structured as follows: First, Section 2 gives detailed insights on methods used for qualitative and quantitative evaluation. Section 3 introduces our evaluation system

[1] https://github.com/allenai/openie-standalone

Proceedings of the First Workshop on Building Linguistically Generalizable NLP Systems, pages 11–18
Copenhagen, Denmark, September 8, 2017.

Name	Type	Domain	Sent.	# Tuple
NYT-222	n-ary	News	222	222
WEB-500	binary	Web/News	500	461
PENN-100	binary	Mixed	100	51
OIE2016	n-ary	Wiki	3200	10359

Table 1: Data sets in RelVis

in a demo walkthrough. We report in Section 4 in-depth insights on our experiment results. Finally, Section 5 concludes with design recommendations for next generation OIE systems.

2 Analysing Open IE Systems

We set up two experiments with four OIE systems STANFORD OPENIE (Angeli et al., 2015), OPENIE 4.2[2], CLAUSIE (Del Corro and Gemulla, 2013) and PREDPAT (White et al., 2016) and four gold standard data sets. The qualitative analysis was done by two human judges, who classified errors in the output of the systems into six categories. Our qualitative analysis includes gold labeled data sets from previous evaluations, shown in Table 1.

2.1 Data sets

Our evaluation process for Open Information Extraction systems should be convenient and comparable. To meet this goal, we deliver supplementary scripts to import commonly used data sets with our evaluation system RelVis. The unified data model enables the user to perform quantitative comparisons and extensive analyses on widely used data sets. We used in our experiments four data sets, see Table 1, of which two feature only binary relations with two arguments. Data sets *NYT-222* and *OIE2016* also contain n-ary relations. These labeled data sets origin from Mesquita et al. (2013) and Stanovsky and Dagan (2016).

2.2 Measuring OIE Systems

A naive way to match a tuple to a gold standard is an *equal match*. Enforcing equal matching of boundaries in text to a gold standard delivers exact results for computing precision. However, this strategy penalizes other, potentially correct, boundary definitions beyond the gold standard. Dealing with multiple OIE systems and their different annotation styles requires a less restrictive matching strategy. A second strategy is a *containment match* where an argument or predicate is considered correct, if it at least contains a gold standard annotation. Hence, spans from the gold standard may be contained (fully) inside the spans of the annotation from the OIE system. However, this strategy may label over-specific tuples as correct and may lead to a lower precision and penalizes binary systems on n-ary data sets.

Therefore we introduce a *relaxed containment strategy* which removes a penalty for wrong boundaries especially for over-specific extractions. This strategy counts an extraction correct, even when the number of arguments doesn't match the gold standard. For example, Stanford OIE, a system that only returns binary OIE tuples, performs well on *NYT-nary (b)*, an n-ary data set and yields large parts of relatively short sentences as one argument. With the relaxed matching strategy Stanford OIEs binary extractions are counted correct as long as they contain all gold standard arguments.

The approach of Mesquita et al. (2013) has simplified the task by replacing all entities in the test set with the words "Europe" and "Asia". In our opinion this decision is contrary to the definition of OpenIE given by Banko et al. (2007) which describes OIE as *"domain-independent discovery of relations extracted from text and readily scales to the diversity and size of the Web corpus."* and may hide or even cause problems in the analysed systems.

Measurements. In our quantitative evaluation we calculate precision, recall and F_2 measure at sentence level. Following Pink et al. (2014), we choose F_2 instead of F_1 measure because it gives the recall a larger impact. The basic intuition is that a high recall of an OIE system is critical to the performance of any downstream application that can apply additional filters.

2.3 Common Error Classes.

Authors of OIE systems distinguish among six major error classes, Table 3 reports errors for our four OIE systems. In the following paragraphs we describe each error class in detail.

Wrong Boundaries. Banko et al. (2007) describe this error as *too large or too small boundaries for an argument or predicate of an OIE extraction*. In each of the four OIE systems we observe wrong boundaries for at least one third of the results. This indicates that OIE systems often

[2]https://github.com/allenai/openie-standalone

fail in generalizing to unseen word distributions. This might be caused by errors in used intermediate structures, such as dependency parses, or overestimation of boundaries. Incorrect boundaries for relation arguments can prohibit fusing, linking or aggregating tuples for the same predicate. As a consequence, an additional system needs to filter out incorrect boundaries which may cause a drastic recall loss.

A solution proposed in the literature is to 'wait' until intermediate systems, such as dependency parser, POS tagger etc., provide an improved generalization. However, this may not always be the case for niche domains, such as medical text or text in enterprise scenarios, where often no labeled corpora for those intermediate systems exist.

Following Arnold et al. (2016a,b) we suggest end-to-end architectures, such as TASTY, an end-to-end named entity recognition and named entity linking system. TASTY leverage stacked deep learning architectures and requires only a few hundred labeled annotations to reach high F-measures in various domains and languages.

Redundant Extraction. In absence of a schema, OIE systems output redundant extractions for the same sentence, such as for the same subject-predicate structure. For example, in the sentence *"Additionally, we included some other relevant results from the 2005 survey in Antwerp."* SIE yields two times the tuple (we, included, other relevant results). These OIE systems are tuned towards high recall and leave the decision to filter out redundant tuples to a downstream application (Del Corro and Gemulla, 2013). The OIE system SIE which returns in extreme cases up to 140 tuples for the same sentence. Our results indicate that this error class has been resolved to a large extent in most systems by filtering and aggregating results from multiple similar extraction rules.

Uninformative Extraction. Following Fader et al. (2011), *uninformative extractions are extractions that omit critical information*. This type of error is caused by improper handling of relation phrases that are expressed by a combination of a verb with a noun, such as light verb constructions (LVCs). Adding syntactic and lexical constraints may solve this problem to certain extent.

Missing Extraction - False Negatives. This class describes relations which were not found by a particular system. According to Fader et al. (2011), missing extractions are often caused by argument-finding heuristics choosing the wrong arguments, or failing to extract all possible arguments. One example is the case of coordinating conjunctions. CIE and OIE can spot certain cases of coordinating conjunctions and do miss fewer tuples. Other sources of this error are lexical constraints filtering out a valid relation phrase, another source are errors in dependency parsing. Overall, we observe a trade-off among OIE systems between utilizing lexical constraints for filtering out uninformative tuples and thereby creating false negatives. Our results indicate that system OIE handles this trade-off slightly better than other systems.

Wrong Extraction. Stanovsky and Dagan (2016) consider a tuple as correct as long as it shares a specified threshold of characters with a gold annotation. However, this policy may lead to emitting large parts of a sentence as one argument and poses additional computation effort to a downstream application. We focus on sentence-level correctness (Mesquita et al., 2013; Angeli et al., 2015) and define a tuple as correct if the following conditions are met:

1. The selected matching strategy yields a match for the predicate.
2. The number of arguments aligns with the gold standard.
3. The selected matching strategy yields a match for all arguments.

This error class is critical since it is not possible to recover from a error of this class and it emits a wrong signal which might trigger additional errors in downstream tasks.

Out of Scope. We observe in Table 3 that our OIE systems yield more correct extractions as recognized by authors of gold data sets. For these additional annotations, we introduce an *out of scope* category. This label does not indicate an error, but it helps us from distinguishing errors of gold labels and additional annotations of a particular OIE system that are not present in the gold standard. Our two judges marked an annotation, in the qualitative evaluation, as out of scope if it is valid and provides an information gain. If marked as out of scope, no other error category is applied to the extraction.

3 The RelVis System

In the following Section, we guide through our OIE benchmark system which was used to perform the quantitative and qualitative analysis. We show how the system can support a user in such sophisticated evaluation processes.

Startup. At system initialisation, RelVis reads gold-annotations. Next, the system stores extraction and gold annotations in a RDBMS from which a web based front end visualizes text data and annotations.

Dashboards for exploring annotations. Now, the user can start exploring results and understanding the behaviour of each system. Figure 1 visualizes in a dashboard example sentences, precision, recall and F_2 scores for each OIE system and for each error class.

Please note, RelVis plots error distributions as a Kiviat diagram and draws bar charts for comparing error class impacts for each OIE system. In addition, the user can export results as tables and CSV files from the database, as shown in Table 3 and Table 2.

Understanding and adding a single annotation. RelVis visualizes OIE extractions on sentence level. Figure 3 shows how the dashboard visualizes example sentences. For each hit by a system, the user can drill down into a single sentence and can understand extraction predicates or arguments. Next, she can dive down into correct or incorrect annotations, can add labels for error classes for incorrect annotations or may leave a comment, see also Figure 2. We permit the user to apply multiple error classes to each part of an annotation, such as a predicate or argument. Next, she can focus on a sentence of interest and can compare extractions between different OIE systems.

We permit the user to update or add new annotations with a BRAT style functionality (Stenetorp et al., 2012), optimized for n-ary OIE relations.

Figure 3 shows a screenshot to illustrate the process. The user selects a sentence to annotate and starts with the first annotation by clicking on the "Add new OIE Relation" button (6). Next, she marks the predicate and arguments in the sentence for her first annotation by selecting them with the cursor and interacting with Button (1) and (2). The system indicates predicates (4) in green and arguments (5) in blue colour.

4 Experiment Results

In a **quantitative evaluation** we report precision, recall and F_2 scores on all four data sets. Table 2 reports overall results for four OIE systems on all four data sets, with the limitation that only a subset of OIE2016, containing 1768 sentences, was available to us. We conduct our experiments with an exact (a) and relaxed (b) containment match strategy.

For the **qualitative evaluation** we execute four OIE systems on 17 sentences of each data set. This resulted in 749 predicted extractions which we evaluate and classify into error categories by two human judges, as shown in Table 3. Additionally, Figure 4 gives an overview of the general performance of all tools over all data sets. We apply a strict containment match strategy in this evaluation. Observing that multiple errors can happen to a single extraction, we assign in these cases more than one error category.

Note, for both experiments, we configure system CIE to binary extraction mode for binary data sets and otherwise in n-ary mode.

4.1 General Findings

We observe no clear overall winner: Each OIE system works best on a particular data set, and no OIE system significantly outperforms on two or more data sets.

Boundary Errors. We observe that an OIE system causes boundary errors often by over- or under-specific argument spans. In more rare cases the source for this error are predicate spans. Both, argument and predicate related errors can be caused by wrong intermediate structures in a particular OIE system. Another source of the problem could be the argument candidate generation, which overestimates the size of an argument span, so that it envelops multiple distinct arguments. Further causes for a boundary error are different annotation styles, which appear among systems as well as among gold standard data sets.

As one possible source for the overall bad results on the NYT-222 dataset, we pinpoint the differing styles of conjunction extraction. Consider a gold standard which expects a single extraction with multiple arguments for the sentence: "*DENVER BRONCOS signed LB Kenny Jackson, DT Garrett Johnson and CB Sam Young.*" like e.g. *signed(DENVER BRONCOS; Kenny Jackson; Garrett Johnson; Sam Young).* Systems CIE and

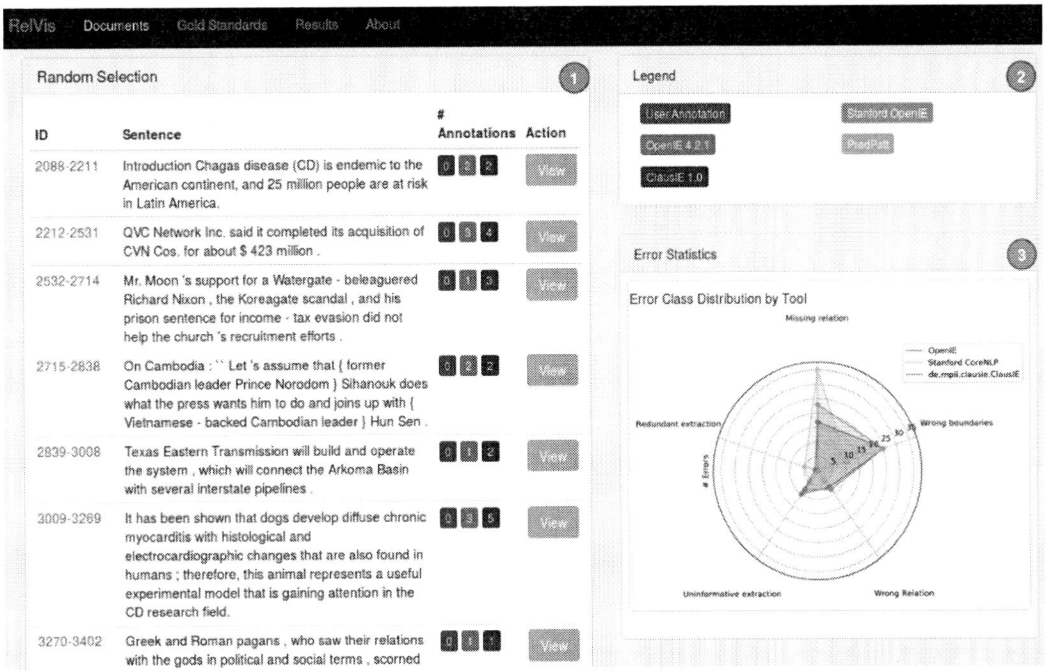

Figure 1: Screenshot of the sentence selection view of RelVis. (1) For each sentence in the document we show text and number of extractions by system. (2) The "Legend panel" denotes various OIE systems with different colours. (3) The lower right hand side shows visualizations of error evaluation statistics.

Dataset	**ClausIE (%)**			**OpenIE 4.2 (%)**			**Stanford OIE (%)**			**PredPatt (%)**		
	P	R	F_2	P	R	F_2	P	R	F_2	P	R	F_2
PENN-100 (a)	4.00	21.15	11.39	12.41	36.54	26.31	**14.85**	**57.69**	**36.58**	6.83	42.30	20.75
PENN-100 (b)	4.00	21.15	11.39	13.07	38.46	27.70	**14.85**	**57.69**	**36.59**	7.76	48.08	23.58
WEB-500 (a)	**16.33**	**46.70**	**34.03**	12.83	19.62	17.74	13.65	40.72	29.16	5.18	13.43	10.19
WEB-500 (b)	**16.33**	**46.70**	**34.03**	13.39	20.47	18.51	13.65	40.72	29.16	6.09	15.78	11.97
NYT-222 (a)	1.64	5.85	3.87	**2.86**	7.66	5.73	0	0	0	2.22	**13.51**	**6.71**
NYT-222 (b)	4.69	16.67	11.03	11.28	30.18	22.60	**13.37**	**73.87**	**38.77**	8.47	51.35	25.51
OIE2016 (a)	14.81	13.67	13.89	**24.85**	**18.69**	**19.67**	0.80	1.49	1.27	7.26	12.39	10.86
OIE2016 (b)	20.38	18.81	19.10	**39.58**	**29.76**	**31.31**	3.83	7.10	6.07	13.52	23.09	20.23

Table 2: Quantitative Evaluation. The (b) variant are results with relaxed containment match strategy and (a) are those with the strict containment strategy.

OIE yield persons and their positions as one large argument in a binary relation: *signed(DENVER BRONCOS; LB Kenny Jackson, DT Garrett Johnson and CB Sam Young.).* On the contrary, System PP implements another style extracting every person of the sample sentence in an own binary relation.

SIE, a binary extraction system, performs surprisingly well on this data set with the relaxed containment match strategy and on *NYT-222 (b)*. With a strict containment match strategy, NYT-222 (a), the system was not able to find a correct extraction, because the data set does not contain binary relations. Using a relaxed containment match strategy, system SIE outperforms all other systems, by extracting large, over-specific arguments. This shifts additional effort for further processing towards downstream applications. This shows the importance of taking boundaries into account in an evaluation. However, system SIE fails on the extraction of OIE2016, which contains more complex sentences, including numerical values and multiple gold annotations in comparison to NYT-222.

Dataset	**NYT-222** (n-ary)				**OIE2016** (n-ary)				**PENN-100** (binary)				**WEB-500** (binary)			
# Relations	17				29				17				17			
	CIE	OIE	PP	SIE	CIE	OIE	PP	SIE	CIE	OIE	PP	SIE	CIE	OIE	PP	SIE
# Predicted	42	35	68	74	28	30	57	91	63	34	61	49	33	22	24	38
# Correct	2	1	**6**	0	8	**12**	6	5	4	8	10	**11**	5	4	3	**10**
# Redundant	0	0	0	**5**	0	0	0	**18**	1	0	0	**4**	**2**	0	0	0
# Uninformative	4	2	**8**	0	2	0	**6**	1	**9**	3	**9**	4	0	0	0	**3**
# Boundaries	11	17	18	**39**	11	11	21	**69**	**14**	5	9	**14**	8	**9**	**9**	**9**
# Wrong	2	1	3	**5**	1	1	**6**	3	3	1	**10**	4	1	**2**	**2**	**2**
# Out of Scope	24	17	**34**	30	7	6	**21**	13	**33**	17	31	18	**19**	8	12	14
# Missed	4	1	**5**	**5**	8	4	7	**12**	**14**	6	6	7	8	3	**11**	6

Table 3: Occurrences of extraction errors found in the qualitative analysis of four OIE systems on 17 sentences drawn from four gold standard datasets. 749 predicted extractions were evaluated in total. Note: multiple errors per predicted extraction are possible and that number of missed extractions is naturally not contained in # Predicted.

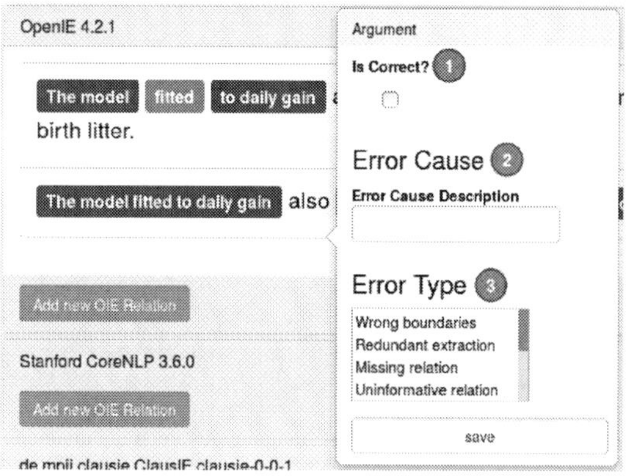

Figure 2: Interface for specifying the correctness (1), comment on error cause (2) and error class (3) of an OIE extraction.

Missed Extractions. Noisy text, wrong intermediate structures and different annotation styles among gold data sets often trigger this error. We report a significant drop in recall for all systems on the WEB-500 dataset compared to PENN-100, except for CIE, see Table 2, even though both data sets show a similar annotation style. However, the WEB-500 data set is quite noisy and contains HTML-character encodings, unfinished sentences or headlines with special characters. Those artifacts cause errors in intermediate structures, like dependency parses or POS tags, which causes the systems to fail. In particular, the n-ary systems OIE or PP do not seem to be robust to such noisy data.

Another source for missed relations is a mismatch between annotation styles. For example, system CIE shows a different style as the gold annotation in PENN-100, NYT-222 and WEB-500 data sets. A closer inspection reveals that CIE's verb centric extraction behaviour handles nominal or adjectival triggered relations (Peng et al., 2014) in a different style as the gold standard data set. Its design triggers inserting an artificial predicate (Del Corro and Gemulla, 2013) which can cause many missed annotations in our evaluation. For example, consider the following sentence: "*At least one potential GEC partner, Matra, insists it isn't interested in Ferranti.*" System CIE extracts the tuple: *is(one potential GEC partner; Matra)*, but the style of the gold standard expects: *partner(GEC; Matra)*. We explain the increase of all scores of system CIE by the larger number of gold annotations, compared to PENN-100, which does not interfere with the annotation style of system CIE.

Wrong and uninformative unary extractions. Wrong extraction errors are in many cases complex and caused by other errors. For example, a boundary error often leads to missing a important information like a negation. Furthermore, we observe problems in the predicate candidate selection process for unary extractions which leads to wrong extractions.

Uninformative extractions are mostly yielded by systems CIE and PP. In many cases, these errors are triggered in possessive relations without resolved co-references or relations with adjectival triggers, e.g. *first(world war)*. To overcome these problems, we suggest to improve filtering for uninformative unary relations, supply additional

Figure 3: Visualization of OIE annotations. The predicate is marked green (4) and arguments blue (5). Buttons for adding a predicate (1) or argument (2) are on top. The button for adding another OIE Annotation (6) is on the bottom. In the top left corner is the delete annotation button (3).

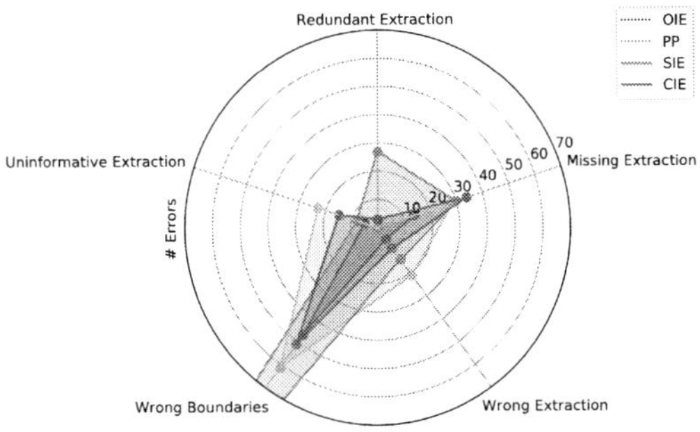

Figure 4: Error occurrence of all OIE systems on 68 sentences of four data sets. Error categories described in ?? are plotted along five axes. The system with the smallest covered area makes the least errors. We crop the diagram at 70 occurrences for easier interpretation. SIE hits 131 times in total the Wrong Boundaries category.

checks for missed negations or important arguments and integrate a co-reference resolution components into next generation OIE systems.

Redundant Extractions Redundant extractions exclusively occur in systems SIE and CIE[3].

4.2 Data set Specific Findings

OIE systems are still designed towards binary tuples. Very first OIE systems had been designed towards emitting binary OIE tuples. Therefore, we observe that all systems achieve a better recall score on the binary data sets when the strict containment strategy is used. This is caused by larger number of possible errors in an n-ary task. Additionally, inconsistent extraction styles for n-ary relations in both, systems and gold standards, cause errors.

Out of Scope. The PENN-100 data set supplies for every sentence just one gold extraction. In most cases it represents a non verbal triggered relation. This leads to many out of scope extractions, because most of the systems perform well in extracting verbal triggered relations. Each OIE system yields out of scope extractions in particular on the NYT-222 data set, which shows that the gold annotations in this data set do not cover capabilities of modern OIE systems.

Data set OIE2016 features the lowest number of out of scope extractions overall. It provides multiple gold annotations per sentence and covers a wide variety of extractions, starting with unary up to 7-ary tuples. System PP yields non verbal triggered unary extractions more often than other systems, which is the reason for its steady high number of out of scope extractions.

5 Conclusion

To our best knowledge this is the first attempt of a comprehensive in-depth error analysis, containing quantitative and qualitative evaluations, of four OIE systems on four data sets. In our future work we will publish our benchmark system RelVis, data sets and adapters under an open source licence for the general OIE community.[4]

Because of the nature of the OIE task, we conclude that there is a lack in stringent annota-

[3] in binary extraction mode

[4] https://github.com/SchmaR/RelVis

tion policies, which makes a comparative analysis but also the design of OIE system often difficult. Moreover, each tested OIE system depends on syntactic taggers that often propagate errors towards the logic for extracting OIE tuples. We also observe fewer errors among binary OIE tuples. This indicates that current OIE systems have not reached an effective design yet for extracting higher order n-ary tuples. Only system PP leverages well researched ideas from normal forms in data base theory in its design.

We suggest designers of next generation OIE systems to test their systems against various data sets, even data sets in idiosyncratic domains not included in this benchmark. Moreover, next generation OIE systems should offer some convenient 'knobs' for tuning it towards common downstream tasks, such as populating a knowledge base or extracting typed relations against a schema.

Acknowledgements

Our work is funded by the German Federal Ministry of Economic Affairs and Energy (BMWi) under grant agreement 01MD16011E (Medical Allround-Care Service Solutions), grant agreement 01MD15010B (Smart Data Web) and by the European Union's Horizon 2020 research and innovation programme under grant agreement No 732328 (FashionBrain).

References

Gabor Angeli, Melvin Johnson Premkumar, and Christopher D. Manning. 2015. Leveraging linguistic structure for open domain information extraction. *Linguistics* (1/24).

Sebastian Arnold, Robert Dziuba, and Alexander Löser. 2016a. TASTY: Interactive Entity Linking As-You-Type. In *COLING Demos 2016*. pages 111–115.

Sebastian Arnold, Felix A. Gers, Torsten Kilias, and Alexander Löser. 2016b. Robust Named Entity Recognition in Idiosyncratic Domains. In *arXiv:1608.06757 [Cs.CL]*.

Michele Banko, Michael J. Cafarella, Stephen Soderland, Matthew Broadhead, and Oren Etzioni. 2007. Open Information Extraction from the Web. In *IJCAI*. volume 7, pages 2670–2676.

Luciano Del Corro and Rainer Gemulla. 2013. Clausie: Clause-based open information extraction. In *Proceedings of the 22nd International Conference on World Wide Web*. International World Wide Web Conferences Steering Committee, pages 355–366.

Anthony Fader, Stephen Soderland, and Oren Etzioni. 2011. Identifying relations for open information extraction. In *Proceedings of the Conference on Empirical Methods in Natural Language Processing*. Association for Computational Linguistics, pages 1535–1545.

Tushar Khot, Ashish Sabharwal, and Peter Clark. 2017. Answering Complex Questions Using Open Information Extraction. *arXiv:1704.05572 [cs]* .

Mausam Mausam. 2016. Open Information Extraction Systems and Downstream Applications. New York.

Filipe Mesquita, Jordan Schmidek, and Denilson Barbosa. 2013. Effectiveness and Efficiency of Open Relation Extraction. In *Proceedings of the 2013 Conference on Empirical Methods in Natural Language Processing*. Association for Computational Linguistics, pages 447–457.

Yifan Peng, Manabu Torii, Cathy H. Wu, and K. Vijay-Shanker. 2014. A generalizable NLP framework for fast development of pattern-based biomedical relation extraction systems. *BMC Bioinformatics* 15:285.

Glen Pink, Joel Nothman, and James R. Curran. 2014. Analysing Recall Loss in Named Entity Slot Filling. In *EMNLP'14*. ACL, Doha, Qatar, pages 820–830.

Gabriel Stanovsky and Ido Dagan. 2016. Creating a Large Benchmark for Open Information Extraction. In *Proceedings of the 2016 Conference on Empirical Methods in Natural Language Processing (EMNLP)*. Association for Computational Linguistics, Austin, Texas, page (to appear).

Gabriel Stanovsky, Ido Dagan, and Mausam. 2015. Open IE as an Intermediate Structure for Semantic Tasks. In *Proceedings of the 53rd Annual Meeting of the Association for Computational Linguistics (ACL 2015)*.

Pontus Stenetorp, Sampo Pyysalo, Goran Topić, Tomoko Ohta, Sophia Ananiadou, and Jun'ichi Tsujii. 2012. Brat: A Web-based Tool for NLP-Assisted Text Annotation. In *Proceedings of the Demonstrations Session at EACL 2012*. Association for Computational Linguistics, Avignon, France.

Aaron Steven White, Drew Reisinger, Keisuke Sakaguchi, Tim Vieira, Sheng Zhang, Rachel Rudinger, Kyle Rawlins, and Benjamin Van Durme. 2016. Universal Decompositional Semantics on Universal Dependencies. In *Proceedings of the 2016 Conference on Empirical Methods in Natural Language Processing*.

Ying Xu, Mi-Young Kim, Kevin Quinn, Randy Goebel, and Denilson Barbosa. 2013. Open Information Extraction with Tree Kernels. In *HLT-NAACL*. pages 868–877.

Massively Multilingual Neural Grapheme-to-Phoneme Conversion

Ben Peters
Saarland University
Saarbrücken, Germany
benzurdopeters@gmail.com

Jon Dehdari and **Josef van Genabith**
DFKI & Saarland University
Saarbrücken, Germany
firstname.lastname@dfki.de

Abstract

Grapheme-to-phoneme conversion (g2p) is necessary for text-to-speech and automatic speech recognition systems. Most g2p systems are monolingual: they require language-specific data or handcrafting of rules. Such systems are difficult to extend to low resource languages, for which data and handcrafted rules are not available. As an alternative, we present a neural sequence-to-sequence approach to g2p which is trained on spelling–pronunciation pairs in hundreds of languages. The system shares a single encoder and decoder across all languages, allowing it to utilize the intrinsic similarities between different writing systems. We show an 11% improvement in phoneme error rate over an approach based on adapting high-resource monolingual g2p models to low-resource languages. Our model is also much more compact relative to previous approaches.

1 Introduction

Accurate grapheme-to-phoneme conversion (g2p) is important for any application that depends on the sometimes inconsistent relationship between spoken and written language. Most prominently, this includes text-to-speech and automatic speech recognition. Most work on g2p has focused on a few languages for which extensive pronunciation data is available (Bisani and Ney, 2008; Novak et al., 2016; Rao et al., 2015; Yao and Zweig, 2015, *inter alia)*. Most languages lack these resources. However, a low resource language's writing system is likely to be similar to the writing systems of languages that do have sufficient pronunciation data. Therefore g2p may be possible for low resource languages if this high resource data can be properly utilized.

We attempt to leverage high resource data by treating g2p as a multisource neural machine translation (NMT) problem. The source sequences for our system are words in the standard orthography in any language. The target sequences are the corresponding representation in the International Phonetic Alphabet (IPA). Our results show that the parameters learned by the shared encoder–decoder are able to exploit the orthographic and phonemic similarities between the various languages in our data.

2 Related Work

2.1 Low Resource g2p

Our approach is similar in goal to Deri and Knight (2016)'s model for adapting high resource g2p models for low resource languages. They trained weighted finite state transducer (wFST) models on a variety of high resource languages, then transferred those models to low resource languages, using a language distance metric to choose which high resource models to use and a phoneme distance metric to map the high resource language's phonemes to the low resource language's phoneme inventory. These distance metrics are computed based on data from Phoible (Moran et al., 2014) and URIEL (Littell et al., 2017).

Other low resource g2p systems have used a strategy of combining multiple models. Schlippe et al. (2014) trained several data-driven g2p systems on varying quantities of monolingual data and combined their outputs with a phoneme-level voting scheme. This led to improvements over the best-performing single system for small quantities of data in some languages. Jyothi and Hasegawa-Johnson (2017) trained recurrent neural networks for small data sets and found that a version of their system that combined the neural network output

Proceedings of the First Workshop on Building Linguistically Generalizable NLP Systems, pages 19–26
Copenhagen, Denmark, September 8, 2017.

with the output of the wFST-based Phonetisaurus system (Novak et al., 2016) did better than either system alone.

A different approach came from Kim and Snyder (2012), who used supervised learning with an undirected graphical model to induce the grapheme–phoneme mappings for languages written in the Latin alphabet. Given a short text in a language, the model predicts the language's orthographic rules. To create phonemic context features from the short text, the model naïvely maps graphemes to IPA symbols written with the same character, and uses the features of these symbols to learn an approximation of the phonotactic constraints of the language. In their experiments, these phonotactic features proved to be more valuable than geographical and genetic features drawn from WALS (Dryer and Haspelmath, 2013).

2.2 Multilingual Neural NLP

In recent years, neural networks have emerged as a common way to use data from several languages in a single system. Google's zero-shot neural machine translation system (Johnson et al., 2016) shares an encoder and decoder across all language pairs. In order to facilitate this multi-way translation, they prepend an artificial token to the beginning of each source sentence at both training and translation time. The token identifies what language the sentence should be translated to. This approach has three benefits: it is far more efficient than building a separate model for each language pair; it allows for translation between languages that share no parallel data; and it improves results on low-resource languages by allowing them to implicitly share parameters with high-resource languages. Our g2p system is inspired by this approach, although it differs in that there is only one target "language", IPA, and the artificial tokens identify the language of the source instead of the language of the target.

Other work has also made use of multilingually-trained neural networks. Phoneme-level polyglot language models (Tsvetkov et al., 2016) train a single model on multiple languages and additionally condition on externally constructed typological data about the language. Östling and Tiedemann (2017) used a similar approach, in which a character-level neural language model is trained on a massively multilingual corpus. A language embedding vector is concatenated to the input at each time step. The language embeddings their system learned correlate closely to the genetic relationships between languages. However, neither of these models was applied to g2p.

3 Grapheme-to-Phoneme

g2p is the problem of converting the orthographic representation of a word into a phonemic representation. A phoneme is an abstract unit of sound which may have different realizations in different contexts. For example, the English phoneme /p/ has two phonetic realizations (or allophones):

- [p^h], as in the word 'pain' [p^h eɪ n]
- [p], as in the word 'Spain' [s p eɪ n]

English speakers without linguistic training often struggle to perceive any difference between these sounds. Writing systems usually do not distinguish between allophones: [p^h] and [p] are both written as ⟨p⟩ in English. The sounds are written differently in languages where they contrast, such as Hindi and Eastern Armenian.

Most writing systems in use today are glottographic, meaning that their symbols encode solely phonological information[1]. But despite being glottographic, in few writing systems do graphemes correspond one-to-one with phonemes. There are cases in which multiple graphemes represent a single phoneme, as in the word *the* in English:

th	e
ð	ə

There are cases in which a single grapheme represents multiple phonemes, such as syllabaries, in which each symbol represents a syllable.

In many languages, there are silent letters, as in the word *hora* in Spanish:

h	o	r	a
-	o	ɾ	a

There are more complicated correspondences, such as the silent *e* in English that affects the pronunciation of the previous vowel, as seen in the pair of words *cape* and *cap*.

It is possible for an orthographic system to have any or all of the above phenomena while remaining unambiguous. However, some orthographic

[1]The Chinese script, in which characters have both phonological form and semantic meaning, is the best-known exception.

systems contain ambiguities. English is well-known for its spelling ambiguities. Abjads, used for Arabic and Hebrew, do not give full representation to vowels.

Consequently, g2p is harder than simply replacing each grapheme symbol with a corresponding phoneme symbol. It is the problem of replacing a grapheme sequence

$$G = g_1, g_2, ..., g_m$$

with a phoneme sequence

$$\Phi = \phi_1, \phi_2, ..., \phi_n$$

where the sequences are not necessarily of the same length. Data-driven g2p is therefore the problem of finding the phoneme sequence that maximizes the likelihood of the grapheme sequence:

$$\hat{\Phi} = \arg\max_{\Phi'} \Pr(\Phi' \mid G)$$

Data-driven approaches are especially useful for problems in which the rules that govern them are complex and difficult to engineer by hand. g2p for languages with ambiguous orthographies is such a problem. Multilingual g2p, in which the various languages have similar but different and possibly contradictory spelling rules, can be seen as an extreme case of that. Therefore, a data-driven sequence-to-sequence model is a natural choice.

4 Methods

4.1 Encoder–Decoder Models

In order to find the best phoneme sequence, we use a neural encoder–decoder model with attention (Bahdanau et al., 2014). The model consists of two main parts: the **encoder** compresses each source grapheme sequence G into a fixed-length vector. The **decoder**, conditioned on this fixed-length vector, generates the output phoneme sequence Φ.

The encoder and decoder are both implemented as recurrent neural networks, which have the advantage of being able to process sequences of arbitrary length and use long histories efficiently. They are trained jointly to minimize cross-entropy on the training data. We had our best results when using a bidirectional encoder, which consists of two separate encoders which process the input in forward and reverse directions. We used long short-term memory units (Hochreiter and Schmidhuber, 1997) for both the encoder and decoder. For the attention mechanism, we used the general global attention architecture described by Luong et al. (2015).

Enc. & dec. model type	LSTM
Attention	General
Enc. & dec. layers	2
Hidden layer size	150
Source embedding size	150
Target embedding size	150
Batch size	64
Optimizer	SGD
Learning rate	1.0
Training epochs	13

Table 1: Hyperparameters for multilingual g2p models

We implemented[2] all models with OpenNMT (Klein et al., 2017). Our hyperparameters, which we determined by experimentation, are listed in Table 1.

4.2 Training Multilingual Models

Presenting pronunciation data in several languages to the network might create problems because different languages have different pronunciation patterns. For example, the string 'real' is pronounced differently in English, German, Spanish, and Portuguese. We solve this problem by prepending each grapheme sequence with an artificial token consisting of the language's ISO 639-3 code enclosed in angle brackets. The English word 'real', for example, would be presented to the system as

`<eng> r e a l`

The artificial token is treated simply as an element of the grapheme sequence. This is similar to the approach taken by Johnson et al. (2016) in their zero-shot NMT system. However, their source-side artificial tokens identify the target language, whereas ours identify the source language. An alternative approach, used by Östling and Tiedemann (2017), would be to concatenate a language embedding to the input at each time step. They do not evaluate their approach on grapheme-to-phoneme conversion.

5 Data

In order to train a neural g2p system, one needs a large quantity of pronunciation data. A standard

[2] https://github.com/bpopeters/mg2p

dataset for g2p is the Carnegie Mellon Pronouncing Dictionary (Lenzo, 2007). However, that is a monolingual English resource, so it is unsuitable for our multilingual task. Instead, we use the multilingual pronunciation corpus[3] collected by Deri and Knight (2016) for all experiments. This corpus consists of spelling–pronunciation pairs extracted from Wiktionary. It is already partitioned into training and test sets. Corpus statistics are presented in Table 2.

In addition to the raw IPA transcriptions extracted from Wiktionary, the corpus provides an automatically cleaned version of transcriptions. Cleaning is a necessary step because web-scraped data is often noisy and may be transcribed at an inconsistent level of detail. The data cleaning used here attempts to make the transcriptions consistent with the phonemic inventories used in Phoible (Moran et al., 2014). When a transcription contains a phoneme that is not in its language's inventory in Phoible, that phoneme is replaced by the phoneme with the most similar articulatory features that is in the language's inventory. Sometimes this cleaning algorithm works well: in the German examples in Table 3, the raw German symbols /χ/ and /ç/ are both converted to /x/. This is useful because the /χ/ in *Ansbach* and the /ç/ in *Kaninchen* are instances of the same phoneme, so their phonemic representations should use the same symbol. However, the cleaning algorithm can also have negative effects on the data quality. For example, the phoneme /ɹ/ is not present in the Phoible inventory for German, but it *is* used in several German transcriptions in the corpus. The cleaning algorithm converts /ɹ/ to /l/ in all German transcriptions, whereas /r/ would be a more reasonable guess. The cleaning algorithm also removes most suprasegmentals, even though these are often an important part of a language's phonology. Developing a more sophisticated procedure for cleaning pronunciation data is a direction for future work, but in this paper we use the corpus's provided cleaned transcriptions in order to ease comparison to previous results.

6 Experiments

We present experiments with two versions of our sequence-to-sequence model. LangID prepends each training, validation, and test sample with

Split	Train	Test
Languages	311	507
Words	631,828	25,894
Scripts	42	45

Table 2: Corpus Statistics

Lang.	Script	Spelling	Cleaned IPA	Raw IPA
deu	Latin	Ansbach	a: n s b a: x	ˈansbaχ
deu	Latin	Kaninchen	k a: n ɪ n x ə n	kaˈni:nçən
eus	Latin	untxi	u n̪ t̪ ʃ ɪ	ˈun.t͡ʃi

Table 3: Example entries from the Wiktionary training corpus

an artificial token identifying the language of the sample. NoLangID omits this token. LangID and NoLangID have identical structure otherwise. To translate the test corpus, we used a beam width of 100. Although this is an unusually wide beam and had negligible performance effects, it was necessary to compute our error metrics.

6.1 Evaluation

We use the following three evaluation metrics:

- Phoneme Error Rate (PER) is the Levenshtein distance between the predicted phoneme sequences and the gold standard phoneme sequences, divided by the length of the gold standard phoneme sequences.

- Word Error Rate (WER) is the percentage of words in which the predicted phoneme sequence does not exactly match the gold standard phoneme sequence.

- Word Error Rate 100 (WER 100) is the percentage of words in the test set for which the correct guess is not in the first 100 guesses of the system.

In system evaluations, WER, WER 100, and PER numbers presented for multiple languages are averaged, weighting each language equally (following Deri and Knight, 2016).

It would be interesting to compute error metrics that incorporate phoneme similarity, such as those proposed by Hixon et al. (2011). PER weights all phoneme errors the same, even though some errors are more harmful than others: /d/ and /k/ are usually contrastive, whereas /d/ and /d̪/ almost never are. Such statistics would be especially interesting for evaluating a multilingual system, because

[3]https://drive.google.com/drive/folders/0B7R_gATfZJ2aWkpSWHpXUklWUmM

different languages often map the same grapheme to phonemes that are only subtly different from each other. However, these statistics have not been widely reported for other g2p systems, so we omit them here.

6.2 Baseline

Results on LangID and NoLangID are compared to the system presented by Deri and Knight (2016), which is identified in our results as wFST. Their results can be divided into two parts:

- High resource results, computed with wFSTs trained on a combination of Wiktionary pronunciation data and g2p rules extracted from Wikipedia IPA Help pages. They report high resource results for 85 languages.
- Adapted results, where they apply various mapping strategies in order to adapt high resource models to other languages. The final adapted results they reported include most of the 85 languages with high resource results, as well as the various languages they were able to adapt them for, for a total of 229 languages. This test set omits 23 of the high resource languages that are written in unique scripts or for which language distance metrics could not be computed.

6.3 Training

We train the LangID and NoLangID versions of our model each on three subsets of the Wiktionary data:

- LangID-High and NoLangID-High: Trained on data from the 85 languages for which Deri and Knight (2016) used non-adapted wFST models.
- LangID-Adapted and NoLangID-Adapted: Trained on data from any of the 229 languages for which they built adapted models. Because many of these languages had no training data at all, the model is actually only trained on data in 157 languages. As is noted above, the Adapted set omits 23 languages which are in the High test set.
- LangID-All and NoLangID-All: Trained on data in all 311 languages in the Wiktionary training corpus.

In order to ease comparison to Deri and Knight's system, we limited our use of the training corpus to 10,000 words per language. We set aside 10 percent of the data in each language for validation, so the maximum number of training words for any language is 9000 for our systems.

6.4 Adapted Results

On the 229 languages for which Deri and Knight (2016) presented their final results, the LangID version of our system outperforms the baseline by a wide margin. The best performance came with the version of our model that was trained on data in all available languages, not just the languages it was tested on. Using a language ID token improves results considerably, but even NoLangID beats the baseline in WER and WER 100. Full results are presented in Table 4.

Model	WER	WER 100	PER
wFST	88.04	69.80	48.01
LangID-High	74.99	46.18	42.64
LangID-Adapted	75.06	46.39	41.77
LangID-All	**74.10**	**43.23**	**37.85**
NoLangID-High	82.14	50.17	54.05
NoLangID-Adapted	85.11	48.24	55.93
NoLangID-All	83.65	47.13	51.87

Table 4: Adapted Results

6.5 High Resource Results

Having shown that our model exceeds the performance of the wFST-adaptation approach, we next compare it to the baseline models for just high resource languages. The wFST models here are purely monolingual – they do not use data adaptation because there is sufficient training data for each of them. Full results are presented in Table 5. We omit models trained on the Adapted languages because they were not trained on high resource languages with unique writing systems, such as Georgian and Greek, and consequently performed very poorly on them.

In contrast to the larger-scale Adapted results, in the High Resource experiments none of the sequence-to-sequence approaches equal the performance of the wFST model in WER and PER, although LangID-High does come close. The LangID models do beat wFST in WER 100. A possible explanation is that a monolingual wFST model will never generate phonemes that are not part of the language's inventory. A multilingual model, on the other hand, could potentially generate phonemes from the inventories of any language it has been trained on.

Even if LangID-High does not present a more accurate result, it does present a more compact one: LangID-High is 15.4 MB, while the combined wFST high resource models are 197.5 MB.

Model	WER	WER 100	PER
wFST	**44.17**	21.97	**14.70**
LangID-High	47.88	**15.50**	16.89
LangID-All	48.76	15.78	17.35
NoLangID-High	69.72	29.24	35.16
NoLangID-All	69.82	29.27	35.47

Table 5: High Resource Results

6.6 Results on Unseen Languages

Finally, we report our models' results on unseen languages in Table 6. The unseen languages are any that are present in the test corpus but absent from the training data. Deri and Knight did not report results specifically on these languages. Although the NoLangID models sometimes do better on WER 100, even here the LangID models have a slight advantage in WER and PER. This is somewhat surprising because the LangID models have not learned embeddings for the language ID tokens of unseen languages. Perhaps negative associations are also being learned, driving the model towards predicting more common pronunciations for unseen languages.

Model	WER	WER 100	PER
LangID-High	**85.94**	58.10	**53.06**
LangID-Adapted	87.78	68.40	65.62
LangID-All	86.27	62.31	54.33
NoLangID-High	88.52	58.21	62.02
NoLangID-Adapted	91.27	57.61	74.07
NoLangID-All	89.96	**56.29**	62.79

Table 6: Results on languages not in the training corpus

7 Discussion

7.1 Language ID Tokens

Adding a language ID token always improves results in cases where an embedding has been learned for that token. The power of these embeddings is demonstrated by what happens when one feeds the same input word to the model with different language tokens, as is seen in Table 7. Impressively, this even works when the source sequence is in the wrong script for the language, as is seen in the entry for Arabic.

Language	**Pronunciation**
English	d ʒ uː æɪ s
German	j ʊ t s ə
Spanish	x w i θ e̞
Italian	d ʒ u i t ʃ e
Portuguese	ʒ w i s ĩ
Turkish	ʒ ʊ ɪ d̪ ʒ ɛ
Arabic	j uː i s

Table 7: The word 'juice' translated by the LangID-All model with various language ID tokens. The incorrect English pronunciation rhymes with the system's result for 'ice'

7.2 Language Embeddings

Because these language ID tokens are so useful, it would be good if they could be effectively estimated for unseen languages. Östling and Tiedemann (2017) found that the language vectors their models learned correlated well to genetic relationships, so it would be interesting to see if the embeddings our source encoder learned for the language ID tokens showed anything similar. In a few cases they do (the languages closest to German in the vector space are Luxembourgish, Bavarian, and Yiddish, all close relatives). However, for the most part the structure of these vectors is not interpretable. Therefore, it would be difficult to estimate the embedding for an unseen language, or to "borrow" the language ID token of a similar language. A more promising way forward is to find a model that uses an externally constructed typological representation of the language.

7.3 Phoneme Embeddings

In contrast to the language embeddings, the phoneme embeddings appear to show many regularities (see Table 8). This is a sign that our multilingual model learns similar embeddings for phonemes that are written with the same grapheme in different languages. These phonemes tend to be phonetically similar to each other.

Perhaps the structure of the phoneme embedding space is what leads to our models' very good performance on WER 100. Even when the model's first predicted pronunciation is not correct, it tends to assign more probability mass to guesses that are more similar to the correct one. Applying some sort of filtering or reranking of the system output might therefore lead to better performance.

Phoneme	Closest phonemes
b	pʰ, β, ɸ
ə	ã, ĕ, ɯ
tʰ	tː, t, t̪
x	χ, ɣ, ħ
y	yː, ʏ, ɪ
ɹ	rˠ, r̪, ɾ

Table 8: Selected phonemes and the most similar phonemes, measured by the cosine similarity of the embeddings learned by the LangID-All model

7.4 Future Work

Because the language ID token is so beneficial to performance, it would be very interesting to find ways to extend a similar benefit to unseen languages. One possible way to do so is with tokens that identify something other than the language, such as typological features about the language's phonemic inventory. This could enable better sharing of resources among languages. Such typological knowledge is readily available in databases like Phoible and WALS for a wide variety of languages. It would be interesting to explore if any of these features is a good predictor of a language's orthographic rules.

It would also be interesting to apply the artificial token approach to other problems besides multilingual g2p. One closely related application is monolingual English g2p. Some of the ambiguity of English spelling is due to the wide variety of loanwords in the language, many of which have unassimilated spellings. Knowing the origins of these loanwords could provide a useful hint for figuring out their pronunciations. The etymology of a word could be tagged in an analogous way to how language ID is tagged in multilingual g2p.

References

Dzmitry Bahdanau, Kyunghyun Cho, and Yoshua Bengio. 2014. Neural machine translation by jointly learning to align and translate. *ArXiv preprint* 1409.0473. http://arxiv.org/abs/1409.0473.

Maximilian Bisani and Hermann Ney. 2008. Joint-sequence models for grapheme-to-phoneme conversion. *Speech communication* 50(5):434–451.

Aliya Deri and Kevin Knight. 2016. Grapheme-to-phoneme models for (almost) any language. In *Proceedings of the 54th Annual Meeting of the Association for Computational Linguistics*. volume 1, pages 399–408.

Matthew S. Dryer and Martin Haspelmath, editors. 2013. *WALS Online*. Max Planck Institute for Evolutionary Anthropology, Leipzig. http://wals.info/.

Ben Hixon, Eric Schneider, and Susan L Epstein. 2011. Phonemic similarity metrics to compare pronunciation methods. In *Twelfth Annual Conference of the International Speech Communication Association (INTERSPEECH)*. Florence, Italy, pages 825–828.

Sepp Hochreiter and Jürgen Schmidhuber. 1997. Long short-term memory. *Neural computation* 9(8):1735–1780.

Melvin Johnson, Mike Schuster, Quoc V. Le, Maxim Krikun, Yonghui Wu, Zhifeng Chen, Nikhil Thorat, Fernanda B. Viégas, Martin Wattenberg, Greg Corrado, Macduff Hughes, and Jeffrey Dean. 2016. Google's multilingual neural machine translation system: Enabling zero-shot translation. *ArXiv preprint* 1611.04558. http://arxiv.org/abs/1611.04558.

Preethi Jyothi and Mark Hasegawa-Johnson. 2017. Low-resource grapheme-to-phoneme conversion using recurrent neural networks. In *Proc. ICASSP*.

Young-Bum Kim and Benjamin Snyder. 2012. Universal grapheme-to-phoneme prediction over Latin alphabets. In *Proceedings of the 2012 Joint Conference on Empirical Methods in Natural Language Processing and Computational Natural Language Learning*. Association for Computational Linguistics, pages 332–343.

G. Klein, Y. Kim, Y. Deng, J. Senellart, and A. M. Rush. 2017. OpenNMT: Open-Source Toolkit for Neural Machine Translation. *ArXiv preprint* https://arxiv.org/abs/1701.02810.

Kevin Lenzo. 2007. The CMU pronouncing dictionary.

Patrick Littell, David Mortensen, Ke Lin, Katherine Kairis, Carlisle Turner, and Lori Levin. 2017. Uriel and lang2vec: Representing languages as typological, geographical, and phylogenetic vectors. In *EACL 2017*. Valencia, Spain, pages 8–14.

Minh-Thang Luong, Hieu Pham, and Christopher D. Manning. 2015. Effective approaches to attention-based neural machine translation. *CoRR* abs/1508.04025. http://arxiv.org/abs/1508.04025.

Steven Moran, Daniel McCloy, and Richard Wright, editors. 2014. *PHOIBLE Online*. Max Planck Institute for Evolutionary Anthropology, Leipzig. http://phoible.org .

Josef Robert Novak, Nobuaki Minematsu, and Keikichi Hirose. 2016. Phonetisaurus: Exploring grapheme-to-phoneme conversion with joint n-gram models in the WFST framework. *Natural Language Engineering* 22(6):907–938.

Robert Östling and Jörg Tiedemann. 2017. Continuous multilinguality with language vectors. *EACL 2017* page 644.

Kanishka Rao, Fuchun Peng, Haşim Sak, and Françoise Beaufays. 2015. Grapheme-to-phoneme conversion using long short-term memory recurrent neural networks. In *International Conference on Acoustics, Speech and Signal Processing (ICASSP)*. pages 4225–4229.

Tim Schlippe, Wolf Quaschningk, and Tanja Schultz. 2014. Combining grapheme-to-phoneme converter outputs for enhanced pronunciation generation in low-resource scenarios. In *International Workshop on Spoken Language Technologies for Under-resourced Languages (SLTU)*. pages 139–145.

Yulia Tsvetkov, Sunayana Sitaram, Manaal Faruqui, Guillaume Lample, Patrick Littell, David Mortensen, Alan W Black, Lori Levin, and Chris Dyer. 2016. Polyglot neural language models: A case study in cross-lingual phonetic representation learning. In *NAACL 2016*. San Diego, California, pages 1357–1366.

Kaisheng Yao and Geoffrey Zweig. 2015. Sequence-to-sequence neural net models for grapheme-to-phoneme conversion. *ArXiv preprint* 1506.00196. http://arxiv.org/abs/1506.00196.

BIBI System Description: Building with CNNs and Breaking with Deep Reinforcement Learning

Yitong Li and **Trevor Cohn** and **Timothy Baldwin**
School of Computing and Information Systems
The University of Melbourne, Australia
yitongl4@student.unimelb.edu.au, {tcohn,tbaldwin}@unimelb.edu.au

Abstract

This paper describes our submission to the sentiment analysis sub-task of "Build It, Break It: The Language Edition (BIBI)", on both the builder and breaker sides. As a builder, we use convolutional neural nets, trained on both phrase and sentence data. As a breaker, we use Q-learning to learn minimal change pairs, and apply a token substitution method automatically. We analyse the results to gauge the robustness of NLP systems.

1 Introduction

Recently, deep learning models have made impressive gains over a range of NLP tasks (Bahdanau et al., 2015; Bitvai and Cohn, 2015). However, recent studies have exposed brittleness in the models, e.g. through adversarial examples (Szegedy et al., 2014; Goodfellow et al., 2015). In these papers, researchers construct cognitively implausible perturbations of raw image inputs to fool state-of-the-art deep learning models. These perturbations are cheap and easy to generate using a "fast-gradient" method, based on analysis of the derivative of the loss with respect to the input.

One issue with the generation of adversarial examples for NLP has been the fact that language data is discrete, and hence difficult to map the continuous outputs of "gradient" methods onto. Furthermore, the perturbations or mutations generated through adversarial methods may be nonsensical to humans. Given this background, the BIBI shared task was devised to study the reliability of NLP systems by generating adversarial test instances, and explicitly training systems to be robust against adversarial test instances. Specifically, the task is based on opposing sets of participants: *builders* aim to build systems robust to different inputs, and *breakers* try to construct instances which will cause the builders' systems to make incorrect predictions.

In this paper, we describe our builder and breaker submissions to the sentiment analysis subtask, which is a sentence-level binary classification task, to predict whether a given review sentence is positive or negative with respect to a given movie. The data set is derived from movie review data (Pang and Lee, 2005) and the Stanford Sentiment Treebank (Socher et al., 2013).

We participated both as a builder and breaker because we are interested in testing the robustness of state-of-the-art neural models, such as convolutional neural networks ("CNNs": Kim (2014)). Also, we were interested in the breaker task as an avenue for exploring how well we can automatically construct adversarial test instances. In the sentiment sub-task, the main job of breakers is to construct minimally-changed pairs that are able to fool the builders' sentiment analysers. For example, the following sentences can be considered to be a minimal pair, with positive (+1) sentiment:

(+1) I love this movie!
(+1) I'm mad for this movie!

2 Approach

Here, we describe the methods we used for both the builder and the breaker. Considering the expense of human judgements, especially for breakers, and the strong desire for the approaches to generalize, we decide to use automatic methods for both tasks.

2.1 Builder System Description

As a builder, we chose to use convolutional neural nets ("CNNs"), based on their strong performance over text classification tasks (Kim, 2014; Zhang et al., 2015). Specifically, we were interested in

Proceedings of the First Workshop on Building Linguistically Generalizable NLP Systems, pages 27–32
Copenhagen, Denmark, September 8, 2017.

testing the robustness of CNNs in NLP applications. We apply Kim (2014)'s model to this task, which is easy and fast to train. We train our models on both phrase-level labelled data (with neutral phrases removed), and sentence-level labelled data; we will refer to these as "phrased-based" and "sentence-based" CNNs, respectively. Below, we present a short outline of the CNN model.

2.1.1 Convolutional Neural Network

The CNN model first operates by embedding each word using a look-up table which is stacked into the sentence matrix $\mathbf{E}_\mathrm{S}$. Then, a 1d convolutional layer is applied to $\mathbf{E}_\mathrm{S}$, which applies a series of filters over each window of t words, with each filter employing a rectifier transform function. In practice, we use window widths of size $t \in \{3, 4, 5\}$, and 128 filters for each size. $\mathrm{MaxPooling}$ is applied to each of the three sizes separately, and the resulting vectors are concatenated to form a fixed-size representation of the given sentence or phrase. Finally, the representation vector is fed into a final $\mathrm{Softmax}$ layer to generate a probability distribution over classification labels.

The model is trained to minimize the loss — defined as the cross-entropy between the ground-truth and the prediction — using the Adam Optimizer (Kingma and Ba, 2015) with a learning rate of 10^{-4} and batch size of 64.

2.2 Breaker System Description

As our breaker, we borrow ideas from generating adversarial examples in computer vision (Szegedy et al., 2014).

Assuming the loss of the system s is accessible and the true label l of the sentence is known, then the given task can be seen as an optimization problem where we simultaneously minimize the loss between the perturbed sentence $h(x)$ and flipped label, and also the distance between them :

$$\min_{\theta_h} \mathcal{L}_s(h(x), \mathbf{1} - l) + \alpha \cdot \mathrm{distance}(h(x), x) \quad (1)$$

Here, system s maps the input sentence x into the label space, and h is the perturbing function.

In text applications, this can be seen as an integer programming problem. Generally, integer optimization is NP-hard (Cunningham et al., 1996), although estimations can be found using heuristic methods, such as simulated annealing. However, considering the complexity of language, solving the given optimization function in only a discrete text space could lead to nonsensical outputs to a human, according to the results of our preliminary experiments [1]. Empirically, this can be attributed to the difficulty of defining an order over a natural language token set, as well as the non-convex nature of the semantic space in natural language generation.

Therefore, instead of optimizing Equation (1) directly, we split the problem into two subtasks: first, we use a reinforcement learning method to learn which tokens or phrases should be changed; and second, we apply a substitution method to those selected tokens, ensuring the quality of the new sentence.

2.2.1 Reinforcement Learning Method

In order to learn the sentiment of a given text, most NLP systems use n-gram feature-based learning methods, including traditional bag-of-words methods (Pang and Lee, 2005) as well as deep learning models (Socher et al., 2013; Kim, 2014). Based on this observation, one intuitive method of fooling the system is to find the "important" tokens within a given sentence, and then modify these to trick a given system into making a wrong prediction.

In our method, we need a baseline system for our breaker method to attack. Here, we choose the sentence-based CNN model, as described above, as an imaginary enemy. For most black-box systems, it is impossible to access the internals of the model and parameters. Therefore, given an input instance, we only use the output of the system, such as the prediction and loss in our method.

To solve this discrete problem, we apply a Reinforcement Learning ("RL") method (Sutton and Barto, 1998), specifically Q-learning (Watkins and Dayan, 1992; Mnih et al., 2013), to model the probability of removing tokens or phrases from a given sentence. Given the token x and an instance of context sentence c, the RL system learns a policy function $\pi(x|c) \rightarrow \{\mathrm{remove}, \mathrm{keep}\}$. We consider each instance as one game, consisting of several rounds. In the first round, c is a randomly-selected sentence, x is the first token in c, and π is the decision process of removing x or not. In each round, π will be learned at the token level, and the resulting sentence will be taken as the new context. The game will be repeated iteratively un-

[1] We used simulated annealing method to solve the given constrain problem directly. The details of results are not presented in this paper.

Builder system	$\mathcal{F}_1$	% of broken examples					
		Total	Average	Breaker 1	Breaker 2	Breaker 3	Breaker 4
Builder 1	**0.528**	25.43	26.76	35.35	22.62	39.79	9.28
RNN (Socher et al., 2013)	0.457	25.96	27.45	34.34	27.38	36.73	11.34
DCNN (Kalchbrenner et al., 2014)	0.483	25.09	25.95	34.84	21.42	36.73	10.82
Bag-of-n-grams	0.510	24.74	25.51	38.38	20.23	36.73	6.70
Phrase-based CNN	0.518	**24.39**	**25.23**	35.35	22.62	33.67	9.28
Sentence-based CNN	0.490	28.57	31.42	39.39	39.28	39.79	7.21

Table 1: The results of builder systems for BIBI blind test set based on average $\mathcal{F}_1$ (higher is better) and percentage of broken cases (lower is better). Details of each builder's system against the breaker's examples are also listed. The best results are indicated in **bold**.

til a max-round limitation is hit. When the game is terminated, the reward of the game will be the loss difference between the original sentence and the residual sentence, where the loss is calculated relative to the baseline system s. Additionally, we use the number of removed tokens as a penalty item in the final reward. The procedure will then randomly select a new instance and start a new game.

For training, we use the standard Deep Q-Learning algorithm, as described in Mnih et al. (2013). For hyper-parameters, max-round is set to 100 and γ to 0.01. The feature extractor ϕ is a multi-layer perceptron over token embeddings, initialized by pre-trained word2vec vectors (Mikolov et al., 2013). The batch size is 128, the initial ϵ is set to 0.3, and the memory size is up to $10,000$. In order to change as few tokens as possible, we empirically set the distance penalty α to 2. The reward is calculated using pre-trained sentence-based CNN, as described above.

2.2.2 Token Substitution Method

Once the algorithm has decided which tokens should be changed, the next move is to find appropriate substitutions. As described above, most systems are based on n-grams, making them very sensitive to unknown tokens. Therefore, we came up with some heuristics.

The first approach draws on our earlier work on learning robust text representations (Li et al., 2017), and is based on synonyms of the given token, based on Princeton WordNet (Miller et al., 1990) using the NLTK API (Bird, 2006). Here, we test possible synonyms, considering their part-of-speech tag, asking the system s whether the loss is reduced after substitution. We also tried to find antonyms that cannot be recognized by the system, causing the predicted sentiment label to not flip. Finally, we add a small amount of human supervision to ensure the fluency of the output sentences, including removal of garbled examples and minor grammar corrections, and to ensure they have the correct sentiment label. To be specific, we discard the "bad-attacked" pairs with loss difference less than 1 empirically. These "bad-attacked" pairs might be able to fool the sentence-based CNN but with low confidence, such that we did not expect them to be good enough to fool other builders' systems. We also filter out sentences with wrong or ambiguous sentiment labels manually. For example, the system sometimes generates expressions with correct grammar but strange sentiment — e.g., *I don't like this lovely movie* which is contradictory and possibly interpretable as ironic — which remains a challenging problem for us to totally eliminate during generation. Last, we slightly modify the outputs to fix minor grammar errors, such as adding or removing the determiner *a* or *the*.

3 Results and Analysis

In this section, we detail the results of our methods, and perform error analysis.

3.1 Builder

The results for the builder systems over the test set are shown in Table 1. To evaluate the robustness of the builder systems, there are two evaluation criteria: average F-score ("$\mathcal{F}_1$") across all breaker test cases (higher is better), and the percentage of breaker test cases that break the system (lower is better). Having a builder fail over only one example in a given minimal pair is considered to have broken that system.

We observed that all the systems are very close over these two criteria. We also see that the phrase-based CNN achieved competitive performance, while the sentence-based CNN is not as robust. This aligns with our intuition, as feeding phrase-labeled data is more precise for model training, and it is much easier for the sentence-based model to overfit the data, according to our analysis. For example, it might consider *the performance is* as a strong positive trigram feature instead of a neutral one, because the expression has higher frequency in the positive training set than that in the negative set. This also occurs for certain entity tokens, such as people's names and places.

To better understand the advantages and disadvantages of CNNs, we perform some error analysis.

One major class of breaker attack is modifying the polarity of a sentence, either syntactically (e.g. by adding/removing *not*) or morphologically (e.g. by adding the prefix *un-*), but actually the CNN is relatively robust to this. We believe the reason is that the n-gram features our CNN learns are more robust representations of words and short phrases. This also explains the performance of the bag-of-n-gram (BoN) system. However, CNN is still slightly better than BoN because CNN only learns the most important features through the MaxPooling operation, and using word embeddings appears to help the model deal with synonyms and antonyms at the word level.

It is almost the same situation when the systems encounter out-of-vocabulary words (OOV). Although OOVs are a significant challenge, we believe they can be overcome by training better sentiment-sensitized word embeddings (Mrkšić et al., 2016), or combining the system with character-level normalization methods (Han and Baldwin, 2011).

However, CNNs are not good at dealing with complex grammatical structures or long-distance dependencies. For instance, changing a comparative from *more than* to *less than* flips the sentiment and is something that humans are sensitized to, but CNNs tend not to capture this difference. Also, CNNs are not sensitive to tense, such as changing the present tense *is* to the past tense *was* to capture pragmatic/connotative effects. For these kinds of examples, we expected to see higher performance among models which better capture syntactic structure, such as recursive neural nets ("RNNs": Socher et al. (2013)) and dynamic convolutional neural networks ("DCNNs": Kalchbrenner et al. (2014)). In practice, however, this was not the case. We cannot conclude the exact reasons without further analysis of these models, however this might indicate that these perceptron-based deep models struggle to capture the logic in human langauge.

To conclude, among traditional models and state-of-the-art deep learning models for sentiment analysis, CNNs are relatively robust.

Test set	Average $\mathcal{F}_1$	Score
Breaker 1	0.79	28.64
Breaker 3	0.84	**31.17**
Breaker 4	0.83	7.48
Breaker 2 (our method)	0.75	19.28

Table 2: The final score of the breakers. The average $\mathcal{F}_1$ over the original sentences of all builders' systems is also listed for each break test set.

3.2 Breaker

Table 2 gives the final scores of the breaker teams. The final score is calculated by averaging the $\mathcal{F}_1$ of each builder's system on the original sentences, multiplied by the percentage of examples that break that system (shown in Table 1).

Overall, about one third of the breakers' examples were able to fool the builders' systems, which is not surprising. On the one hand this is encouraging, in that, without taking the untapped test cases into consideration, each builder can handle more than half of the break examples. On the other hand, still nearly one third of the break sentences cannot be handled by state-of-the-art statistical models.

For our breaking approach, we observe that all the builders' systems have lower $\mathcal{F}_1$ on our test set, indicating that our method tends to generate difficult sentences, where systems might have lower confidence. Actually, in our final submission, we only chose 42 pairs as the final break data from among the 521 test data instances provided by the organisers, as the rest of the generated pairs were removed due to low confidence or bad quality sentences. This unfortunately indicates that our automatic method cannot be applied to all examples, making our approach limited in application. Therefore, we can't really conclude that our automatic approach is a success, and we should explore more flexible approaches in the future. However, the approach itself still achieves a break rate higher than the error rate on the original test set. Additionally, our method breaks the sentence-based CNN — which our RL model is built on — with 39.28% break rate.

Based on error analysis over the broken examples, we found that using tokens with opposite sentiment in an example worked across builder systems in most cases. For instance, *if you love to waste your time* could confuse most systems because of the contrast between *love* and *waste time*, because they indicate opposing sentiment in isolation, while the phrase itself is focused on *waste time*, which is very difficult for most NLP systems to understand. This indicates that representations of natural language may be doing more than simply adding or transforming the word embeddings, and instead non-compositionally transforming the logic structure of the sentence.

Also, attacking words or phrases which are ambiguous between positive and negative sentiment is also a potentially effective approach. For example, *rock* is used predominantly in positive-sentiment contexts, in reference to jewels or strong/reliable people, meaning that systems are likely to learn that it has exclusively positive sentiment due to bias in the training set. However, when the negative substitution phrase *on the rocks* (meaning "in trouble") is used, the builders' systems might still predict the idiom as having positive sentiment.

Based on these observations, we can conclude that state-of-the-art statistical models have only minimal "understanding" of natural language. The examples we showed above are relatively simple, but in real cases, they can be more complex. And we are not even considering the ambiguity of language or tone of the language in different contexts. To summarize, our approach provides a method to study the robustness of modern NLP systems over a sentiment analysis task. Our results demonstrate that NLP systems are still far from turning the corner to real language understanding.

4 Conclusions

In this paper, we have described our builder and breaker systems, in the context of the BIBI the Language Edition shared task. We built sentiment analysis systems using text-based convolutional neural networks, trained on either phrase- and sentence-level data. Also, we used reinforcement learning and substitution methods to generate adversarial test examples automatically. We performed error analysis to better understand the robustness of statistical NLP models.

Acknowledgements

We would like to thank the three anonymous reviewers for their helpful feedback and suggestions, and to Meng Fang for assisting with the implementation of the RL system.

References

Dzmitry Bahdanau, Kyunghyun Cho, and Yoshua Bengio. 2015. Neural machine translation by jointly learning to align and translate. In *Proceedings of the International Conference on Learning Representations*.

Steven Bird. 2006. NLTK: The natural language toolkit. In *Proceedings of the COLING/ACL 2006 Interactive Presentation Sessions*. pages 69–72.

Zsolt Bitvai and Trevor Cohn. 2015. Non-linear text regression with a deep convolutional neural network. In *Proceedings of the 53rd Annual Meeting of the Association for Computational Linguistics and the 7th International Joint Conference on Natural Language Processing (Volume 2: Short Papers)*. pages 180–185.

William H Cunningham, S Thomas McCormick, and Maurice Queyranne. 1996. *Integer Programming and Combinatorial Optimization*. Springer.

Ian J. Goodfellow, Jonathon Shlens, and Christian Szegedy. 2015. Explaining and harnessing adversarial examples. In *Proceedings of the International Conference on Learning Representations*.

Bo Han and Timothy Baldwin. 2011. Lexical normalisation of short text messages: Makn sens a #twitter. In *Proceedings of the 49th Annual Meeting of the Association for Computational Linguistics: Human Language Technologies*. pages 368–378.

Nal Kalchbrenner, Edward Grefenstette, and Phil Blunsom. 2014. A convolutional neural network for modelling sentences. In *Proceedings of the 52nd Annual Meeting of the Association for Computational Linguistics (Volume 1: Long Papers)*. pages 655–665.

Yoon Kim. 2014. Convolutional neural networks for sentence classification. In *Proceedings of the 2014 Conference on Empirical Methods in Natural Language Processing*. pages 1746–1751.

Diederik P. Kingma and Jimmy Ba. 2015. Adam: A method for stochastic optimization. In *Proceedings of the International Conference on Learning Representations*.

Yitong Li, Trevor Cohn, and Timothy Baldwin. 2017. Robust training under linguistic adversity. In *Proceedings of the 15th Conference of the European Chapter of the Association for Computational Linguistics: Volume 2, Short Papers*. pages 21–27.

Tomas Mikolov, Ilya Sutskever, Kai Chen, Greg S. Corrado, and Jeff Dean. 2013. Distributed representations of words and phrases and their compositionality. In *Advances in Neural Information Processing Systems 26*. pages 3111–3119.

George A. Miller, Richard Beckwith, Christiane Fellbaum, Derek Gross, and Katherine J. Miller. 1990. Introduction to WordNet: an on-line lexical database. *International Journal of Lexicography* 3(4):235–244.

Volodymyr Mnih, Koray Kavukcuoglu, David Silver, Alex Graves, Ioannis Antonoglou, Daan Wierstra, and Martin A. Riedmiller. 2013. Playing atari with deep reinforcement learning. *CoRR* abs/1312.5602.

Nikola Mrkšić, Diarmuid Ó Séaghdha, Blaise Thomson, Milica Gašić, Lina M. Rojas-Barahona, Pei-Hao Su, David Vandyke, Tsung-Hsien Wen, and Steve Young. 2016. Counter-fitting word vectors to linguistic constraints. In *Proceedings of the 2016 Conference of the North American Chapter of the Association for Computational Linguistics: Human Language Technologies*. pages 142–148.

Bo Pang and Lillian Lee. 2005. Seeing stars: Exploiting class relationships for sentiment categorization with respect to rating scales. In *Proceedings of the 43rd Annual Meeting of the Association for Computational Linguistics*. pages 115–124.

Richard Socher, Alex Perelygin, Jean Wu, Jason Chuang, Christopher D. Manning, Andrew Ng, and Christopher Potts. 2013. Recursive deep models for semantic compositionality over a sentiment treebank. In *Proceedings of the 2013 Conference on Empirical Methods in Natural Language Processing*. pages 1631–1642.

Richard S Sutton and Andrew G Barto. 1998. *Reinforcement Learning: An Introduction*. MIT Press, Cambridge, USA.

Christian Szegedy, Wojciech Zaremba, Ilya Sutskever, Joan Bruna, Dumitru Erhan, Ian Goodfellow, and Rob Fergus. 2014. Intriguing properties of neural networks. In *Proceedings of the International Conference on Learning Representations*.

Christopher JCH Watkins and Peter Dayan. 1992. Q-learning. *Machine learning* 8(3-4):279–292.

Xiang Zhang, Junbo Jake Zhao, and Yann LeCun. 2015. Character-level convolutional networks for text classification. In *Advances in Neural Information Processing Systems 28: Annual Conference on Neural Information Processing Systems 2015, December 7-12, 2015, Montreal, Quebec, Canada*. pages 649–657.

Breaking NLP: Using Morphosyntax, Semantics, Pragmatics and World Knowledge to Fool Sentiment Analysis Systems

Taylor Mahler, Willy Cheung, Micha Elsner,
David King, Marie-Catherine de Marneffe,
Cory Shain, Symon Stevens-Guille and **Michael White**
The Ohio State University
mahler.38@osu.edu

Abstract

This paper describes our "breaker" submission to the 2017 EMNLP "Build It Break It" shared task on sentiment analysis. In order to cause the "builder" systems to make incorrect predictions, we edited items in the blind test data according to linguistically interpretable strategies that allow us to assess the ease with which the builder systems learn various components of linguistic structure. On the whole, our submitted pairs break all systems at a high rate (72.6%), indicating that sentiment analysis as an NLP task may still have a lot of ground to cover. Of the breaker strategies that we consider, we find our semantic and pragmatic manipulations to pose the most substantial difficulties for the builder systems.

1 Introduction

This paper describes our submission to the 2017 EMNLP "Build It Break It" shared task on sentiment analysis, in which we constructed minimal pairs of sentences designed to fool sentiment analysis systems that would participate in the task. One member of the pair existed in the blind test data, and the other member was a minimally edited version of the first member designed to cause the systems to make an incorrect prediction on exactly one of the two. The edits were made according to four broad, linguistically interpretable strategies: altering syntactic or morphological structure, changing the semantics of the sentence, exploiting pragmatic principles, and including content that can only be understood with sufficient world knowledge. Some of our changes were designed to fool bag-of-words models, others used more complex structures to try to fool more sophisticated systems relying on parsing and/or compositional methods. Our submitted pairs broke the builder systems at a high rate (72.6%) on average, and our overall weighted F_1 score as defined by the shared task (28.67) puts us in second place out of the four breaker submissions.

2 Strategies

Our edits to the original sentences can be categorized under four broad categories: morphological and syntactic change, semantic change, pragmatic change, and use of world knowledge to determine the meaning. This categorization scheme draws on the definitions used across the field of linguistics; we give a more precise definition of each category below.

In each example, we indicate how our team judged the sentence in terms of sentiment ('+' for positive sentiment and '–' for negative sentiment); these labels were viewed as "gold" by the organizers. In each pair, the first sentence is the original one, the second our constructed test case. The test cases highlighted below were especially effective at breaking builders' systems (i.e., most or all of the systems predicted the wrong sentiment, where superscripts ‡, †, and ⋆ indicates that all but 2, 1, and 0 systems predicted the wrong sentiment).

Figure 1 shows a histogram of minimal pairs by strategy in our submission.

2.1 Morphological and Syntactic Strategies

Edits involving syntactic and morphological changes included the addition or removal of negation, as well as comparatives. Both syntactic negation and comparatives exhibit co-occurrence restrictions, one of the canonical diagnostics for syntactic properties (?). These restrictions can be seen in (1) for lexical negation. *Not* in this case syntactically selects a verb phrase (VP); the VP can stand alone as it does in our edited version

Proceedings of the First Workshop on Building Linguistically Generalizable NLP Systems, pages 33–39
Copenhagen, Denmark, September 8, 2017. ©2017 Association for Computational Linguistics

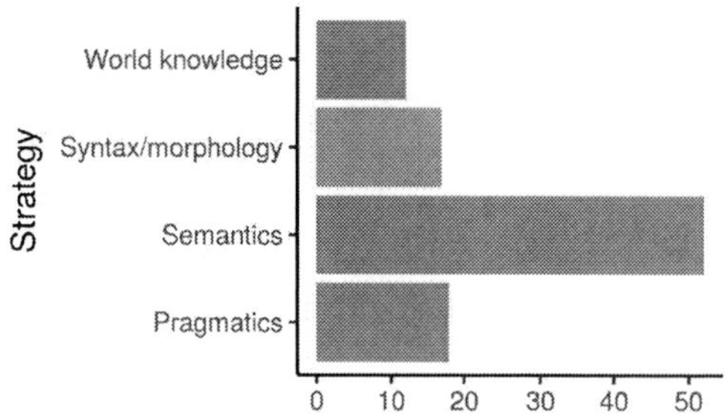

Figure 1: Number of submitted test pairs by strategy.

of the sentence precisely because *not* imposes a co-occurrence restriction on the VP rather than vice versa. Moreover, except in sentence-final emphatic cases, *not* imposes linear order restrictions, appearing prior to the VP.[1] Although there is some dialectical variation, our edited version of the sentence that uses *quite* without negation is slightly degraded, frequently judged as archaic or pretentious, and would also receive some level of additional phonological emphasis on *quite*, which is unavailable from text alone.[2] By contrast, *not quite* is a common expression arguably far less subject to judgment variation.

(1) - In the structure of his screenplay Ross has taken a risk, and he has **not** quite brought it off.
    + ‡In the structure of his screenplay Ross has taken a risk, and has quite brought it off.

Comparatives also impose co-occurrence restrictions, subcategorizing for both an object to be compared and another to be compared to. In the literature on comparatives, the *-er* morpheme is often taken to affect scopal relations beyond its surface position; moreover, *-er* is taken to be analogous to *more* in its semantics and to likewise subcategorize for a(n expression of) degree (**??**). Nonetheless, the present case is still morphological insofar as it is the distribution of *-er*, as opposed to *less*, that distinguishes the members of the pair—the former must morphologically compose with another expression, the latter need not.[3] Removing an adjective for the morpheme to compose with is then predicted to produce different corresponding semantic–and consequently sentiment—effects, as in (2):

(2) + School of Rock made me laugh **harder** than any movie I've seen this year.
    – *School of Rock made me laugh **less** than any movie I've seen this year.

Finally, we introduced negation morphologically, by the addition of derivational morphemes, as in (3) and (4):

(3) + [A] great big ball of entertainment ...
    – ‡[A] great big ball of **anti**-entertainment ...

(4) + A remarkably convincing examination of heroism, hero worship, and the seductive allure of villainy.
    – ‡A remarkably **un**convincing examination of heroism, hero worship, and the seductive allure of villainy.

We hypothesized that minimal edits to these constructions could introduce semantic scope resolution difficulties for NLP systems and cause them to mis-classify the overall sentiment. Our intuition is that NLP applications can perform sentiment analysis reasonably well on the original sentences. By only editing words which carry semantic operators, a sentiment analysis system with no model of semantics or the scope of semantic operators would be unable to capture the change in sentiment.

2.2 Semantic Strategies

Semantic edits are those that that affect the truth conditions of the expression. One might object

[1] Compare with an emphatic case, which is also usually accompanied by emphatic phonological stress on the expression of negation:

He quite brought it off, not!

[2] By dialectical variation we have in mind the differences between e.g., certain American and Canadian dialects of English, as opposed to British dialects, for which some of the present authors have personal attestation of such sorts of utterance.

[3] Compare:

**School of Rock made me laugh lesser than any movie I've seen this year.*

School of Rock gave me fewer laughs than any movie I've seen this year.

Note that according to (**?**)[527] '*less* and *as* differ from *more* only in the nature of the ordering relation they impose', where the ordering relation is over degrees.

that all of the examples in the other strategies have a semantic component.[4] This is true, but our semantics-specific strategy targets semantic information that is independent of the morphology or the syntax of the expressions, while the other strategies explicitly exploit morphological and semantic information that may e.g., alter scope information.

Most edits involving semantic changes altered the sentiment by introducing or modifying an operator that is not straightforward negation, such as *too*, *enough* and *only*. Since these words shift a sentiment's polarity without altering the rest of the sentence, we hypothesized that sentiment analysis systems that are not sensitive to these shifts would mislabel sentences with these edits:

(5) – Aiming to join the Jerry Bruckheimer/Michael Bay school of American movie war games, Stealth is just **too** dumb to make the grade.
+ †Aiming to join the Jerry Bruckheimer/Michael Bay school of American movie war games, Stealth is just dumb **enough** to make the grade.

Another strategy that shifts sentiment polarity without modifications to the original sentence involves embedding clauses or predicates under various semantic operators. In (6), for example, embedding the original clause under *tell* diminishes the author's commitment to that clause. Further, adding *I simply can't see why* reverses the positive sentiment of that original clause.

(6) + An exceptional science fiction film.
– †**Many have told me this is** an exceptional science fiction film**, but I simply can't see why.**

In (7), changing the modal *could* to *should* subtly reverses the sentiment.

(7) – This quirky, snarky contemporary fairy tale could have been a family blockbuster.
+ †This quirky, snarky contemporary fairy tale **should** have been a family blockbuster.

In (8), we embedded the verb phrase from the original sentence under *keep trying*, thus implying that the event described by the complement of *keep trying* has not happened.

(8) + The two featured females offset these distractions by having so much apparent fun that it becomes contagious.
– ‡The two featured females **keep trying to** offset these distractions by having so much apparent fun that it becomes contagious.

Finally, some edits were purely lexical and thus belong to the domain of lexical semantics. In these cases, a single word or multi-word expression carrying the sentiment was changed, as in (9) where we used an antonym.

(9) – This movie plays like they were reading [Roger Ebert's] little movie glossary and they took every cliche in there.
+ *This movie plays like they were reading [Roger Ebert's] little movie glossary and they **avoided** every cliche in there.

In some cases where the genre of the film was mentioned, we simply changed it. Since different genres are intended to have different effects, what counts as positive and negative depends on the genre of the movie. For instance, in (10), the description of the experience of the film does not match the intended effects of a romantic comedy, but it does match those of a horror film.

(10) – The Break-Up, a grim excuse for a romantic comedy, is basically an hour and 45 minutes spent in the company of two unpleasant people during a miserable time in their lives.
+ †The Break-Up, **a grimly compelling horror film**, is basically an hour and 45 minutes spent in the company of two unpleasant people during a miserable time in their lives.

While it might be argued that manipulation of genre is a world knowledge strategy, since the sentiment of these sentences depends crucially on understanding the lexical meaning of the word that

[4] This also goes some way to explaining the success of the semantic strategies in general, since they are in part exploited by the other strategies.

indicates the genre, we classify genre manipulation as a semantic strategy.

2.3 Pragmatic Strategies

Pragmatic strategies make use of inferences which go beyond the literal compositional meaning of the words, relying on knowledge of general principles of human communication, but *not* on extra-linguistic and contextual knowledge. Since most NLP applications lack the information necessary to make use of pragmatics as robustly as humans do, we exploited a variety of pragmatic principles to either create or convey an impression of sarcasm. In the simplest case, we used scare quotes to convey sarcasm, changing the sentiment from positive to negative, as in (11).

(11) + Russell is terrific as coach Herb Brooks.
– *Russell is "terrific" as coach Herb Brooks.

This seemingly simple manipulation actually proved quite difficult for the builder systems. Both pairs we submitted that used this strategy broke all six builder systems.

In other examples, we created Gricean conversational implicatures (?). For instance, our constructed sentence in (12) flouts the Gricean maxim of quantity by providing too little information, implicating that a more informative statement praising the film could not be made because it would be false, and violate the maxim of quality. While there's nothing overtly negative in our constructed sentence in (12), it nonetheless conveys a negative sentiment.

(12) + I think it's a sweet film.
– †I think it's a film.

Our edited sentence in (13) flouts the maxim of relation by providing information that is not relevant in a movie review, implicating that a relevant, positive statement could not be made because it would be false (again violating the maxim of quality).

(13) + The **performances** are uniformly superb.
– *The **marketing** was uniformly superb.

A final pragmatic strategy involved cases where two phrases were conjoined with *but*. Often the sentiment of the second conjunct is also the sentiment of the entire sentence. In such cases, reversing the order of the conjuncts can also reverse the sentiment of the entire sentence, as in the constructed example in (14).

(14) – The sentiments are right on the money, but the execution never quite filled me with holiday cheer.
+ ‡The execution never quite filled me with holiday cheer, but the sentiments are right on the money.

2.4 World Knowledge Strategies

Most NLP applications have a limited understanding of world knowledge. To exploit this shortcoming, we edited sentences so that world knowledge crucially affected the sentiment of the sentence. Arguably, the world knowledge strategies are pragmatic in nature since pragmatics is typically taken to involve meaning that is contributed by context (?) . However, we categorize these strategies separately since the inferences exploiting world knowledge strategies crucially rely on extra-linguistic knowledge.

Many of the sentences we edited using this strategy involved a comparison. We edited such sentences so that knowledge about the standard of comparison was crucial for determining the sentiment. In some cases, the standard of comparison was a named entity, such as a film or an actor. In (15), the negative sentiment arises as a result of the comparison to a Jim Carrey film, which is not intended to be creepy and calibrated:

(15) + Unfolds with the creepy elegance and carefully calibrated precision of a Dario Argento horror film.
– *Unfolds with all the creepy elegance and carefully calibrated precision of a Jim Carrey comedy film.

In other cases, the comparison was metaphorical, and we manipulated the sentiment by altering the nature of the comparison itself. For instance, understanding that the constructed sentence in (16) is negative requires knowledge about the weight of bricks.

(16) + As pretty and light as a **feather** on the wind.
– †As pretty and light as a **brick** on the wind.

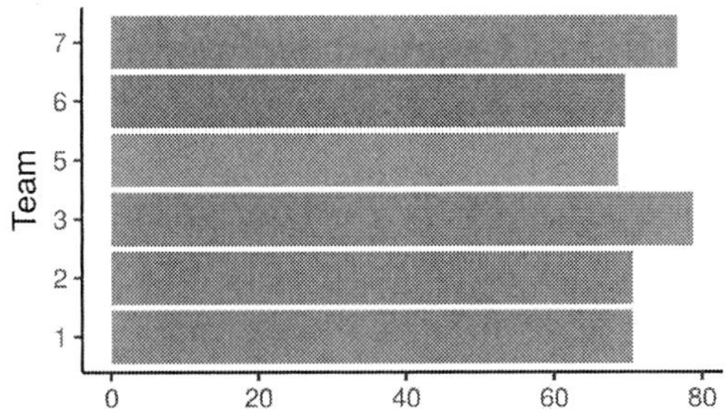

Figure 2: Percent break (out of all submitted pairs) by system.

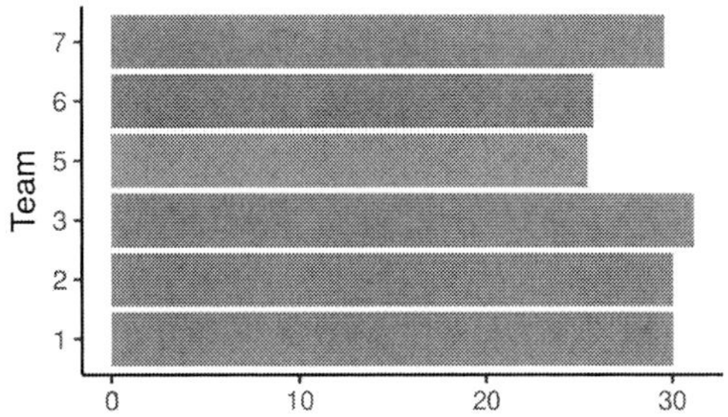

Figure 3: Weighted F_1 score by builder system on our 99 pairs.

We also manipulated the perspective from which a particular sentiment is conveyed. If the review praises something as being valued by individuals that are held in poor regard, then the sentiment is likely to be negative, despite the apparent praise. For example, understanding that the second sentence in (17) is negative requires knowing that racists are (generally) not well regarded.

(17) + An inspiring story for **teens and up**.
– *An inspiring story for **racists**.

Since most NLP applications do not know, for example, that Jim Carrey films are not intended to be creepy and calibrated, that bricks are heavier than feathers, and that one should not blindly follow the recommendations of racists, we predicted that computers would show lower performance when analyzing sentiment in these cases.

3 Results

Following the shared task's definition, a minimal pair is considered to "break" a builder system if the system makes a correct prediction for one member of the pair and an incorrect prediction for the other. The shared task also defines a weighted F_1 score for breaker teams as the F_1 of the builder system on the original sentences of the blind test set, multiplied by the percent of builder sentences on which the breaker team made an incorrect prediction.

We submitted 99 breaker pairs in total. We obtained a mean percent break across systems of 72.6%,[5] and the mean weighted F_1 across systems on our pairs was 28.67, placing us second in terms of this metric out of the four breaker teams in the

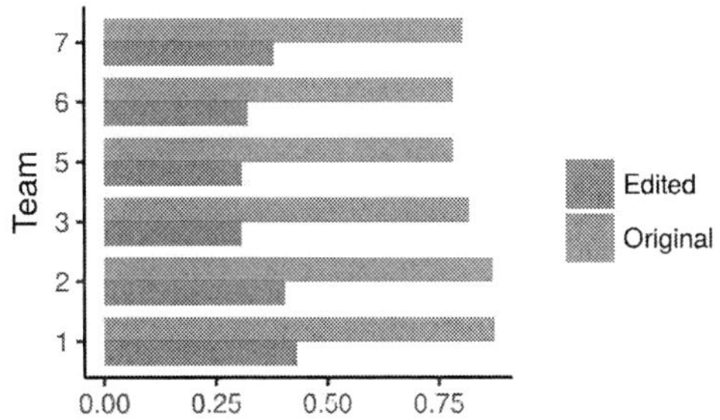

Figure 4: Raw F_1 by system on original vs. edited examples

shared task. Figures 2 and 3 shows percent break and weighted F_1 respectively by system. System 5 had the lowest percent break on our submitted test cases, while system 3 had the highest.

In figure 4, we also present the raw F_1 scores by system on original vs. edited sentences. As is clear in the figure, our edits dramatically compromise classification accuracy across all systems.[6] Note that while Teams 5 and 6 perform well in terms of percent break shown in Figure 2, they have some of the lowest raw F_1 scores shown in Figure 4. This suggests that the strong break rate scores for these systems are driven by pairs in which both items are incorrectly classified, which are not considered to be breaks by the task definition.

Figure 5 provides overall percent break by strategy. Our pragmatic manipulations had the highest percent break while our world-knowledge-based manipulations had the lowest.

In addition to breaks, there were also pairs on which the systems got both sentences wrong. For

[5] I.e., the percent of all submitted pairs (99) that resulted in a break for that system as defined by the shared task.

[6] Although in principle breaker teams were allowed to submit edits designed to make classification easier, almost all of our submitted edits were designed to make classification harder.

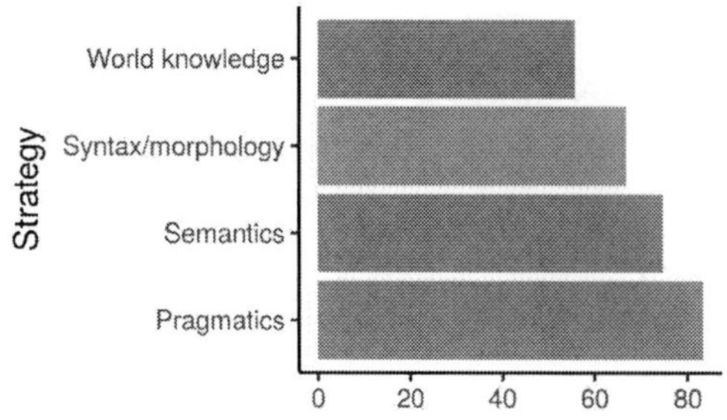

Figure 5: Percent break (out of all submitted pairs) by strategy.

the most part, these appear to have been "neutral" labels (neither negative nor positive) used by the neural network teams (systems 5 and 6). Since neutral sentiment is not part of the gold label space, this appears to have been an error on the part of these systems. Note that as a consequence, the percent break for systems 5 and 6 was lower than it might have been otherwise.

We did not significance test differences in performance between systems or strategies because (1) the same items were shared across builder systems and were therefore not truly independent and (2) we were unsure whether our examples constituted a representative sample of naturally-occurring hard cases. Thus, while our findings are suggestive of the kinds of linguistic phenomena that pose difficulties for automatic sentiment analysis, we are unable to draw firmer conclusions based on this limited sample.

4 Ineffective test cases

In §2, we presented examples of test cases that tended to break the builder systems; here we briefly analyze the *ineffective* test cases (i.e., test cases that most or all of the systems got right) in hopes of evaluating where our test cases failed to break systems and/or where existing systems tended to predict the correct sentiment.

As shown in §3, our test cases yielded a generally high break rate across systems. In fact, of the 99 test cases we submitted, 72 broke more than half of the systems. Of the remaining 27 test cases on which at least half of the systems did not break, 12 were same-sentiment pairs (out of 12 total in our submission). In general these involved attempts to use one of the strategies discussed above to make a positive or negative classification more difficult. However, we appear to have left enough residual evidence of the source sentiment in the edited cases to allow most systems to make the correct decision. In addition, 8 of the 27 test cases involved lexical semantic manipulations, and 7 involved world knowledge, suggesting that these kinds of nuances may not have been as difficult for sentiment analysis systems as we had hypothesized.

The four cases below failed to break any system:

(18) – Unlike Raiders of the Lost Ark, which this movie wants so desperately to be, there's nothing here to engage the brain along with the eyeballs.
– This movie is not like Raiders of the Lost Ark, which this movie wants so desperately to be.

(19) – This is one of the worst movies of the year.
– This is not one of the worst movies of the year.

(20) – Big on slogans, but low on personality.
– Low on personality, but big on slogans.

(21) + The less you know about this movie before seeing it — and you really should see it — the better.
– The less you know about this movie, the better.

Three out of four of these failed examples were same-sentiment (negative-negative) minimal pairs. The fourth removes the positive-sentiment parataxis *and you really should see it* to flip the overall sentiment. In all these cases, there remain words with likely negative sentiment that might short-circuit the difficulty that the edit was intended to introduce (*wants so desperately to*, *worst movies of the year*, *low on personality*, and *the less you know ... the better*). Thus, in hindsight, it would have been better to exclude such examples, since it is not clear whether builder systems succeeded on them by correctly analyzing them or simply by detecting the negative-sentiment-bearing keywords.

5 Discussion

Our results, and those of the shared task in general, serve to highlight the distance which even sophisticated, modern sentiment analysis systems have yet to cover, particularly in terms of semantic and pragmatic analysis. Moreover, changes that broke the systems were often comparatively slight; just as image classification systems can be vulnerable to adversarial examples that look very similar to the originals (?), sentiment analysis systems may be fooled by changes to single words or morphemes. In many cases, of course, our strategies for constructing these examples drew on previous knowledge about hard problems, for instance in parsing (?) and the detection of irony in text (?). Nonetheless, a concrete set of examples of these problems may help developers to create more robust systems in the future.

For sets of constructed examples like ours to be useful, they should contain enough instances of each construction to reliably indicate a system's capabilities. Looking towards the future, we hope that the next iteration of the contest will use a larger test section so that more examples can be created. Many of our strategies targeted particular constructions or idioms (for instance, right-node raising or concrete metaphors), and it was difficult to create many instances of these due to sparsity in the 521-example dataset. We found it difficult to create 100 examples as requested; in fact, two other breaker teams (including the one with the winning F-score) created only half as many.

A related issue is that of naturalness. Although we tried to make our examples sound like real sentences from movie reviews, we had no empirical way to check how well we did. It is probably easier to break NLP algorithms with *unnatural* or out-of-domain examples; although we hope we have not done so, in future, we would like to find better ways to make sure.

Acknowledgments

We would like to thank Julia Papke, Ramon Reyes-Padilla, and Marten van Schijndel for contributing minimal pairs, as well as three anonymous reviewers for helpful feedback and suggestions.

References

Alfred V. Aho and Jeffrey D. Ullman. 1972. *The Theory of Parsing, Translation and Compiling*, volume 1. Prentice-Hall, Englewood Cliffs, NJ.

American Psychological Association. 1983. *Publications Manual*. American Psychological Association, Washington, DC.

Ashok K. Chandra, Dexter C. Kozen, and Larry J. Stockmeyer. 1981. Alternation. *Journal of the Association for Computing Machinery* 28(1):114–133. https://doi.org/10.1145/322234.322243.

Dan Gusfield. 1997. *Algorithms on Strings, Trees and Sequences*. Cambridge University Press, Cambridge, UK.

An Adaptable Lexical Simplification Architecture for Major Ibero-Romance Languages

Daniel Ferrés, Horacio Saggion
Large Scale Text Understanding Systems Lab
TALN - DTIC
Universitat Pompeu Fabra
08018 Barcelona, Spain
daniel.ferres@upf.edu
horacio.saggion@upf.edu

Xavier Gómez Guinovart
TALG Group
Universidade de Vigo
E-36310 Vigo, Spain
xgg@uvigo.es

Abstract

Lexical Simplification is the task of reducing the lexical complexity of textual documents by replacing difficult words with easier to read (or understand) expressions while preserving the original meaning. The development of robust pipelined multilingual architectures able to adapt to new languages is of paramount importance in lexical simplification. This paper describes and evaluates a modular hybrid linguistic-statistical Lexical Simplifier that deals with the four major Ibero-Romance Languages: Spanish, Portuguese, Catalan, and Galician. The architecture of the system is the same for the four languages addressed, only the language resources used during simplification are language specific.

1 Introduction

Text Simplification (Saggion, 2017) should facilitate the adaptation of available and future textual material making texts more accessible. Although there are many characteristics which can be modified in order to make information more readable or understandable, automatic text simplification has usually be concerned with two different tasks: lexical simplification and syntactic simplification. Lexical Simplification, the focus of the present work, aims at replacing difficult words with easier synonyms, while preserving the meaning of the original text. Lexical simplifiers can be potentially useful for different target groups with specific accessibility issues ranging from children, second language (L2) learners (Petersen and Ostendorf, 2007), low literacy readers (Aluísio and Gasperin, 2010), people with cognitive disabilities (Saggion et al., 2015), among others. Moreover, different natural languages have been object of automatic text simplification studies including English (Biran et al., 2011; Ferrés et al., 2016), Spanish (Bott et al., 2012), and Portuguese (Specia, 2010) just to name a few. To the best of our knowledge no previous research has addressed the issue of language adaptation of lexical simplification systems. We here present an approach to Lexical Simplification in the four major Ibero-Romance Languages: Catalan (ca), Galician (gl), Portuguese (pt), and Spanish (es) using the same underlying architecture. The Ibero-Romance languages (also known as Iberian Languages) are the ones that developed on the Iberian Peninsula and in southern France. These languages, that share high lexical similarities, are currently spoken by more than 750 million people around the world. The research and development of Textual Simplification systems for languages with high lexical similarities among them, such as Ibero-Romance languages with about and above 85% of lexical similarities (see Table 1), has the advantage of producing processing and lexical resources that can be easily adapted semi-automatically.

	ca	es	pt
ca	-	85%	85%
es	85%	-	89%
pt	85%	89%	-

Table 1: Lexical similarity between the 3 major Ibero-Romance languages according to Ethnologue[1]. Data for Galician were not available.

The lexical simplifier presented in this paper has been developed following current robust, corpus-based approaches (Biran et al., 2011; Bott et al., 2012; Ferrés et al., 2016) combined with a hybrid Morphological Generator that uses both a wide-coverage lexicon freely available and a

[1] www.ethnologue.com

Proceedings of the First Workshop on Building Linguistically Generalizable NLP Systems, pages 40–47
Copenhagen, Denmark, September 8, 2017.

Decision-Trees based algorithm, and an easy to adapt rule-based context re-writting module. The availability of such a robust multilingual generator is key for inflecting words, which in the rich morphological languages addressed is extremely important.

The contributions of this paper can be summarized as follows:

- The first multilingual lexical simplification architecture.[2]
- The first system to address lexical simplification for Catalan and Galician.
- A well-established evaluation of the adequacy and simplicity of the simplifications based on native speakers' assessment.

The rest of the paper is organized as follows: in Section 2 we describe the related work. The architecture of the lexical simplifier and its evaluation are described in Sections 3 and 4. After a detailed discussion in Section 5, the paper is concluded at Section 6 with some conclusions and further work.

2 Related Work

Work on Lexical Simplification for English began in the PSET project (Devlin and Tait, 1998). The authors used WordNet to identify synonyms and calculated their relative difficulty using Kucera-Francis frequencies in the Oxford Psycholinguistic Database. De Belder and Moens (De Belder and Moens, 2010) combined this methodology with a latent words language model which modeled both language in terms of word sequences and the contextual meaning of words. Wikipedia has also been used in lexical simplification studies. Biran et al. (Biran et al., 2011) used word frequencies in English Wikipedia and Simple English Wikipedia (SEW) to calculate their difficulty while Yatskar et al. (Yatskar et al., 2010) used SEW edit histories to identify the simplify operations. More recently, (Glavaš and Štajner, 2015) proposed a simplification method based on current distributional lexical semantics approaches for languages for which lexical resources are scarce. The same line of research is followed by (Paetzold, 2016) who additionally includes a retrofitting mechanism to better distinguish between synonyms and antonyms (Faruqui et al., 2015).

[2]Not based on parallel or comparable corpora.

Regarding Lexical Simplification in Ibero-Romance languages, there are five systems reported in the literature for Spanish and Portuguese:

- LexSiS (Bott et al., 2012) is a lexical simplifier for Spanish. LexSiS uses a word vector model derived from a 8M word corpus of Spanish text extracted from the Web for Word Sense Disambiguation with the Spanish OpenThesaurus as a source for finding candidate synonyms of complex words. Lexical realization is carried out using a dictionary and hand-crafted rules.

- PorSimples is a lexical simplifier for Portuguese (Aluísio and Gasperin, 2010). PorSimples uses the Unitex-PB dictionary and the MXPOST POS tagger for lemmatization and PoS tagging. Complex word detection is performed with a dictionary of simple words. The TeP 2.0 thesaurus and PAPEL lexical ontology were used to find a set of synonyms without the use of Word Sense Disambiguation. The lexical simplicity order of synonyms is determined with word frequencies obtained through Google API.

- Specia (2010) used the Moses toolkit for phrase-based Statistical Machine Translation (SMT) and a corpus of about 4,483 sentences (3,383 for training, 500 for tuning, and 500 for test) in order to learn how to simplify sentences in Brazilian Portuguese.

- Stajner (2014) also used phrase-based SMT for lexical simplification in Spanish. She built language models derived from the Spanish Europarl corpus and used 700 sentence pairs for training, 100 sentence pairs for development, and three test sets for testing (of 50, 50, and 100 sentences).

- Baeza-Yates et al. (2015) presented CASSA a lexical simplifier for Spanish. CASSA uses the Google Books Ngram Corpus to find the frequency of target words and its contexts and uses this information for disambiguation. The Spanish OpenThesaurus (version 2) is used to obtain synonyms and web frequencies are used for disambiguation and lexical simplicity. No morphological realization is performed in this system.

3 Lexical Simplifier

The Lexical Simplification architecture allows to simplify words (common nouns, verbs, adjectives, and adverbs) in context. The architecture follows an approach similar to the YATS lexical simplifier (Ferrés et al., 2016). The simplifier has the following phases (executed sequentially): (i) Document Analysis, (ii) Complex Words Detection, (iii) WSD, (iv) Synonyms Ranking, and (v) Language Realization (see the architecture of the system in Figure 1). The Document Analysis phase uses the FreeLing 4.0[3] system (Padró and Stanilovsky, 2012) to perform tokenization, sentence splitting, part-of-speech (PoS) tagging, lemmatization, and Named Entity Recognition.

3.1 Complex Word Detection

The Complex Word Detection (CWD) phase is carried out to identify target words to be substituted. The procedure identifies a word as complex when the frequency count of word forms or lemmas in a given frequency list extracted from a corpus is below a certain threshold value (i.e. w is complex if $w_{frequency} \leq theshold$).

The frequency lists that can be used separately by this phase are: 1) the Wikipedia forms counts, 2) the Wikipedia extracted lemmas with associated PoS tags[4] (only common nouns, verbs, adjectives and adverbs are extracted), and 3) the OpenSubtitles 2016 words full frequency list[5].

lang	Wikipedia		OpenSubtitles2016
	#lemmas&PoS	#forms	#forms
ca	2,571,667	1,306,344	65,687
es	6,844,698	2,645,049	1,882,198
gl	1,130,788	630,318	73,808
pt	4,829,021	1,975,973	477,456

Table 2: Statistics of the frequency lists.

For example, Table 3 shows how commonly used noun lemmas such as *hand* (having the forms "mà" in Catalan (ca) ,"mano" in Spanish (es) ,"man" in Galician (gl),"mão" in Potuguese (pt)) and *lawyer* ("advocat" (ca), "abogado" (es), "avogado" (gl), "advogado" (pt)) have much more counts in Wikipedia than less common lemmas such as *democracy* ("democràcia" (ca), "democracia" (es,gl,pt)) and *gastronomy* ("gastronomia" (ca), "gastronomía" (es,gl,pt)).

lang	#counts			
	hand	lawyer	democracy	gastronomy
ca	24,936	4,994	3,055	1,163
es	60,271	20,432	11,485	6,850
gl	4,878	2,003	1,084	457
pt	29,556	12,267	4,443	1,172

Table 3: Example of some word lemmas counts in Wikipedia.

In order to obtain a threshold for each language for the Complex Word Detection phase the following procedure has been applied: 1) A set of pairs <complex word, simpler synonym> (such as <novelist,writer> or <tenor,singer>) has been extracted from the LexSiS Gold (Bott et al., 2012) (Spanish) and the PorSimples FSP (Aluísio et al., 2008) (Portuguese) corpora: 102 pairs have been extracted from the LexSiS Gold corpora and 279 from the PorSimples FSP. 2) The 102 pairs in Spanish from LexSiS Gold have been automatically translated to Catalan and manually revised. In order to create a set of 100 pairs from Galician some pairs have been extracted from the 279 pairs in Portuguese and some new pairs have been manually added. 3) A measure of complex word detection accuracy that involves the use of both the complex word and the simpler synonym for each pair has been created. This measure has been called *accuracy complexS* and calculates the ratio of pairs in which its complex word component has been detected as complex word according to the threshold and at the same time the simpler synonym component has been detected as simple word according to the threshold. On the other hand, another measure called *accuracy complex* has been defined as the ratio of pairs in which its complex word component has been detected as complex word according to the threshold. 4) The measure *accuracy complexS* has been used to tune the thresholds of each language: a) a set of thresholds that have been found empirically to maximize the *accuracy complexS* is obtained by automatic testing through intervals of thresholds (the frequency list is divided in a set of 50,000 intervals of thresholds ranging from 0 to the maximum frequency in the corpus) , b) from the selected set of thresholds another subset is obtained by selecting the ones with the best *accuracy complex* measure results, c) finally the higher threshold from the last subset is chosen to be the complex word threshold

[3] http://nlp.cs.upc.edu/freeling

[4] The tools to extract the lemmas and PoS tags from Wikipedia are explained in the Section 3.2.

[5] https://github.com/hermitdave/FrequencyWords

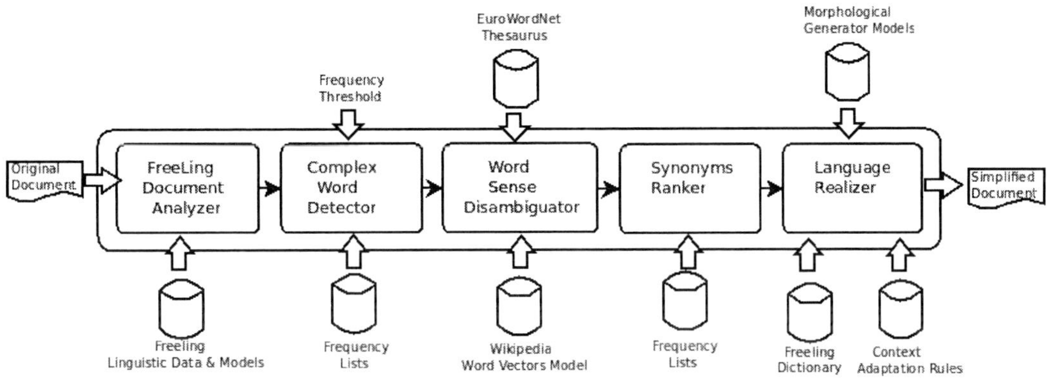

Figure 1: System Architecture.

for the language.

The results of applying this tuning procedure using the 3 frequency lists over the 4 set pairs in each languages are shown in Table 4. The best thresholds for both *accuracy complexS* and *accuracy complex* are obtained by the Wikipedia forms frequency lists (for *ca*, *es*, and *gl*) and with the OpenSubtitles 2016 frequency list for *pt*.

lang	frequency list	accuracy complex	accuracy complexS
ca	cawiki (lemma)	0.7500	0.5200
	cawiki (form)	**0.8000**	**0.6200**
	opensubtitles	0.7100	0.5300
es	eswiki (lemma)	0.7524	0.5346
	eswiki (form)	**0.8613**	**0.6237**
	opensubtitles	0.8613	0.5940
gl	glwiki (lemma)	0.5154	0.2371
	glwiki (form)	**0.6082**	**0.4845**
	opensubtitles	0.2886	0.2164
pt	ptwiki (lemma)	0.7562	0.2258
	ptwiki (form)	0.7132	0.4767
	opensubtitles	**0.8530**	**0.6308**

Table 4: Complex word tunning: best accuracies for threshold computation.

3.2 Word Sense Disambiguation

The WSD algorithm used is based on the Vector Space Model (Turney and Pantel, 2010) approach for lexical semantics which has been previously used in Lexical Simplification (Biran et al., 2011; Bott et al., 2012). The set of language-dependent thesaurus used for WSD was extracted from FreeLing 4.0 data which is derived from Multilingual Central Repository (MCR) 3.0[6] (release 2012). Each thesaurus contains a set of synonyms and its associated set of senses with related synonyms (see the number of entries and senses of each language thesaurus in Table 5).

The WSD algorithm uses a word vectors model derived from a large text collection from which a word vector for each word in the thesaurus is created by collecting co-occurring word lemmas of the word in N-window contexts (only nouns, verbs, adjectives, and adverbs). Then, a common vector is computed for each of the word senses of a given target word (lemma and PoS) by adding the vectors of all words in each sense. When a complex word is detected, the WSD algorithm computes the cosine distance between the context vector computed from the words of the complex word context (at sentence level) and the word vectors of each sense from the model. The word sense selected is the one with the lowest cosine distance between its word vector in the model and the context vector of the complex word in the sentence or document to simplify.

lang	EuroWordNet #entries	EuroWordNet #senses	Wikipedia #docs.	Wikipedia #words
ca	46,555	64,095	450,885	124.5M
es	36,571	50,397	1,061,535	349M
gl	23,058	26,009	221,422	36.2M
pt	35,635	45,737	956,553	203M

Table 5: Statistics of the EuroWordNet thesaurus and the Wikipedia collections processed.

The Catalan, Galician, Portuguese and Spanish Wikipedia dumps were used to extract the word vectors model. The plain text of the documents was extracted using the WikiExtractor[7] tool (see in Table 5 the number of documents and words ex-

[6] http://adimen.si.ehu.es/web/MCR/

[7] http://medialab.di.unipi.it/wiki/Wikipedia_Extractor

tracted from each Wikipedia dump). The FreeLing 3.1 NLP tool was used to extract the lemmas and PoS tags of each word, from a 11-word window (5 content words to each side of the target word).

3.3 Synonyms Ranking

The Synonyms Ranking phase ranks synonyms by their lexical simplicity and finds the simplest and most appropriate synonym word for the given context (Specia et al., 2012). The simplicity measure implemented is the word form (or lemma) frequency (i.e. more frequent is simpler) (Saggion, 2017). The frequency lists that can be used are the ones described in the CWD phase.

3.4 Language Realization

The Language Realization phase generates the correct inflected forms of the final selected synonyms lemmas and the other lemmas of the context. It has two phases: i) a context-independent Morphological Generator and ii) a rule-based Context Adaptator. The Morphological Generation system combines lexicon-based generation and predictions from Decision-Trees (see (Ferrés et al., 2017) for a more detailed description of this system). The lexicons used are the FreeLing[8] (Padró and Stanilovsky, 2012) morphological dictionaries for *ca,es,gl* and *pt* (see in Table 6 more details about these dictionaries). The Decision Trees algorithm used to predict the inflected form is the J48 algorithm from the WEKA[9] data mining tool. This algorithm is only used when the lexicon has no inflection for a pair <lemma,PoS>. The J48 model can predict the sequence of edit operations that can transform an unseen pair <lemma,PoS> to an inflected form.

	Freeling Data		Training Data	
lang	#lemmas	#forms	corpus	#tokens
ca	66,168	642,437	CoNLL09	390,302
es	70,150	669,216	CoNLL09	427,442
gl	45,674	570,912	UD_Galician	79,329
pt	94,444	1,214,090	Bosque 8.0	232,600

Table 6: Morphological Generation training data statistics.

The J48 training algorithm uses morphological and lemma based features including the Levenshtein edit distance between lemmas and word forms to create a model for each lexical category. The learning datasets used were: the CoNLL2009 shared Task[10] Catalan and Spanish training datasets, the Bosque 8.0 corpus tagged with EAGLES tagset[11], and the Galician UD treebank[12] based on the CTG corpus[13].

The Morphological Generator was evaluated independently using the following corpora to test: CoNLL2009 Shared task evaluation dataset for Catalan (53,016 tokens) and Spanish (50,635 tokens), the Galician UD test set for Galician (29,748 tokens) and the Portuguese UD test set for Portuguese (5,499 tokens)[14]. The results (see Table 8) show that the Morphological Generator configuration that uses both FreeLing and J48 achieves high performance with accuracies over or close to 99% in almost all cases with the exception of the verbs in Spanish and Portuguese which obtained a 95.77% and 95.49% of accuracy respectively and the adjectives in Portuguese with a 94.34%.

The Context Adaptation phase generates the correct inflected forms of the lemmas in the context of the substituted complex word in case that it is needed an adaptation due to the morphological features of the substitute synonym. In the Ibero-Romance languages treated there are 3 cases of this kind (not all these cases are treated yet by our system):

1) adaptation of articles, pronouns and prepositions due to an ortographic variation of the substituted synonym (only in *ca* and *gl* languages): e.g. apostrophize determiners in *ca* ("el marit/l'home" (husband/man)), pronominal accusative changes in *gl* ("relatouno / díxoo" ("relatou+no" – (s)he related it / "díxo+o" – (s)he said it)).

2) adaptation of determiners (and pronouns) due to a morphological change of noun gender: as an example in the 4 languages the word "sovereignty" ("sobirania" (*ca*), "soberanía" (*es,gl*) "soberania" (*pt*) can be substituted for its synonym "power" ("poder" (*ca,es,gl,pt*)) but if a determiner precedes the word then it has to change its gender ("la" to "el" (*ca,es*) , "a" to "o" (*gl,pt*)).

3) adaptation of verbs (and adjectives) due to the need of gender concordance: e.g the verb "administer" ("administrat/administrada" (*ca*), "ad-

[8] http://nlp.lsi.upc.edu/freeling/

[9] http://www.cs.waikato.ac.nz/~ml/weka/

[10] http://ufal.mff.cuni.cz/conll2009-st/

[11] http://www.linguateca.pt/floresta/corpus.html

[12] http://universaldependencies.org

[13] http://sli.uvigo.gal/CTG/

[14] Both Galician and Portuguese UD datasets taken from http://hdl.handle.net/11234/1-1983

	system	Simplicity scale					Adequacy scale				
		1	2	3	4	5	1	2	3	4	5
ca	MFS	1.35%	15.59%	15.25%	34.91%	32.88%	11.86%	16.27%	8.13%	22.71%	41.01%
	simplifier	2.37%	17.62%	14.57%	27.11%	38.30%	7.79%	21.01%	9.83%	21.01%	40.33%
es	MFS	6.77%	14.57%	15.93%	25.76%	36.94%	15.93%	14.57%	9.49%	17.96%	42.03%
	simplifier	8.13 %	11.52%	23.05%	27.11%	30.16%	18.64%	15.93%	5.76%	15.93%	43.72%
gl	MFS	13.94%	15.30%	23.46%	25.51%	21.76%	16.94%	16.94%	14.23%	31.86%	20.00%
	simplifier	17.62%	16.94%	21.01%	26.44%	17.96%	21.35%	20.33%	10.84%	26.77%	20.67%
pt	MFS	5.6%	17.2%	25.42%	27.79%	23.38%	12.54%	15.93%	12.88%	30.84%	27.79%
	simplifier	8.84%	14.28%	24.48%	31.97%	20.40%	14.96%	18.70%	13.26%	27.55%	25.51%

Table 7: Evaluation of simplicity and adequacy over a subset of 50 randomly selected sentences from the Wikipedia and simplified by the lexical simplifier and the MFS baseline.

lang.	Algorithm	Noun	Verb	Adj	Adv
ca	FreeLing (C)	72.19	96.63	77.63	77.48
	J48	**99.56**	98.42	98.76	**100**
	FreeLing+J48	99.53	**99.39**	**99.47**	**100**
es	FreeLing (C)	72.60	95.03	76.21	72.89
	J48	99.80	94.32	99.24	98.51
	FreeLing+J48	**99.84**	**95.77**	**99.44**	**98.57**
gl	FreeLing (C)	90.31	97.95	94.46	88.82
	J48	99.70	96.95	99.39	97.76
	FreeLing+J48	**99.97**	**99.96**	**99.91**	**98.10**
pt	FreeLing (C)	88.31	91.12	60.00	82.60
	J48	**98.75**	95.21	93.47	**99.56**
	FreeLing+J48	**98.75**	**95.49**	**94.34**	**99.56**

Table 8: Results of the evaluation in accuracy (%) of the Morphological Generator configurations. Note that in the Freeling configuration the accuracy means coverage (C) because the lexicon cannot predict unseen <lemma,PoS> pairs.

ministrado/administrada" (*es,gl,pt*)) in the sentence "the medicine was administered to the patient", has to be conjugated in concordance with the synonym that substitutes the word "medicine".

4 Evaluation

The evaluation has been realized using a lexical simplifier system with the best parameters obtained in the complex word detection tuning phase and these frequency lists have been also used in the Synonyms Ranking phase. We performed manual evaluation of the simplifier relying on 7 different proficient human judges for each language evaluated,[15] who assessed our system with respect to adequacy and simplicity. The evaluation dataset was created from a set of sentences of the Wikipedia which had at least one non-monosemous complex word and 2 synonyms and less than 26 tokens (Named Entities included as tokens). Then this dataset was simplified and the sentences that had only one lexical simplification were selected[16]. A set of 50 sentences with more than 18 tokens was randomly selected from this set of lexically simplified sentences. The participants were presented with the source sentence from the Wikipedia followed by either a sentence simplified by the full system or a by a baseline version of the system that uses the most frequent synonym (MFS) of all senses as WSD. Simplicity was measured using a five point rating scale that indicates how much simpler was the simplified sentence w.r.t the original (high numbers indicate simpler). Adequacy was also measured using a five point rating scale that indicates if the simplified sentences keeps the same meaning (high numbers indicate more adequacy). Table 7 shows the evaluation results in simplicity and adequacy.

5 Discussion

The Complex Word Detection phase presented uses frequency thresholding over frequency lists extracted from corpora. The motivation of using such methodology is to have a generic method to detect complex words for average adult people that can be easily adaptable to several languages and requiring only textual corpora. Obviously this method has some problems: 1) the extraction of frequencies from huge corpora may rely on sets of documents with unbalanced, over-represented or under-represented domains that could suppose to generate high frequencies for real complex words or low frequencies for simple words, 2) the threshold tunning process is sensible to the semantic complexity level of the list word pairs used, and this could led to generate complex word detections useful only for certain groups of people.

In order to test if some simple words could have low frequencies in the corpora (Spanish Wikipedia) with respect to the threshold used for

[15]Graduates and university undergraduate students. None of them developed the simplifier.

[16]This step was performed to avoid interference of multiple simplifications.

the Wikipedia forms frequency list we used a list of subjective estimation of Age of Acquisition (AoA) words in Spanish (Alonso et al., 2015). The average AoA score for each word was based on 50 individual responses on a scale from 1 to 11 (indicating the age that this word was acquired). A set of 2,307 words estimated to be acquired at an age below 6 years (so supposing that these words have to be very simple) has been used for this test. Using the best threshold obtained in tuning procedure to estimate complex words has resulted in that 829 of these words (35.87%) were correctly not detected as complex words but 1,455 (62.99%) were incorrectly detected as complex words and 25 were not found (0.37%). This means that at least in Spanish (of the 4 languages used the one which has more documents in the Wikipedia) some words that are really simple such as "sopa" (soup), "to fish" (pescar), and "veinticinco" (twenty-five) among others have been detected as complex words.

In order to solve these problems, besides of increasing and balancing the corpora, the modularity of the resource allow these kind of solutions: 1) both the threshold and the frequency list files can be edited manually and change the frequency of those words, 2) generating manually or semi-automatically frequency lists of complex words or simple words that can be generic or adapted to specific target groups, and 3) combine both corpus-based frequency lists and manually generated. Previous competitive approaches to complex word identification are many times based on word frequency thresholding as we implement here (see (Wrobel, 2016) who obtained the best F-score in the recent Complex Word Identification task (Paetzold and Specia, 2016))

The results obtained through subjective manual assessment by native evaluators show that both the MFS baseline and the full simplifier obtain more than 50% of positive results (scores 4 and 5 in the five-point rating scale) in simplicity and adequacy a for *ca*,*es*, and *pt* and more than 40% for *gl*. These results mean that both the system and the MFS baseline can be useful for lexical simplification but the large percentage of negative results in adequacy (scores 1 and 2 in the five-point rating scales) indicates that more research is needed to avoid errors of meaning preservation. The reported errors in adequacy and the fact that the simplifier generally does not perform better than the MFS baseline point that the WSD algorithm and/or its resources need to be improved.

In general Lexical Simplification systems do not deal with Morphological Generation, for example CASSA (Baeza-Yates et al., 2015) has not morphological realization component, LexSiS morphological realization (Bott et al., 2012) is limited to a dictionary and set of handcrafted rules. Simplification systems based on machine translation (Specia, 2010; Stajner, 2014) generate words based on parallel/comparable original and simplified datasets being therefor limited in coverage (e.g. words not observed in the dataset will not be properly generated). Our approach instead is robust in terms of coverage and easily adapted to new languages with similar characteristics (e.g. Italian, French). It is worth notice that both approaches we present here: the baseline and our simplifier both take advantage of the morphological realization component. Moreover, the only module that is not used by the baseline is the Word Sense Disambiguator.

6 Conclusion

Automatic Lexical Simplification is a task that requires very complex and advanced resources in both Natural Language Processing and Natural Language Generation fields. In this paper we have presented a modular automatic Lexical Simplifier system that can deal with the four major Ibero-Romance Languages: Spanish, Portuguese, Catalan, and Galician. The experiments presented in this paper show that the corpus-based approaches tried, despite of being useful for generic prediction, are not yet sufficient to deal with the complexities of the task and manual effort from linguistic experts to create specific resources for the task is needed.

Future research includes: a) experiments with other available datasets, b) use more advanced vector representations (e.g. embeddings), c) update the thesaurus data of MCR 3.0 from release 2012 to release 2016 and apply some manual or automatic revision to prune or mark loosely related synonyms, d) experiments with the CHILDES corpus for complex word detection, and e) porting the system to other similar major Romance languages such as French, Italian and Romanian.

Acknowledgements

This work is (partly) supported by the Spanish Ministry of Economy and Competitiveness under the Maria de Maeztu Units of Excellence Programme (MDM-2015-0502) and by the TUNER project (TIN2015-65308-C5-5-R and TIN2015-65308-C5-1-R, MINECO/FEDER, UE).

References

María Angeles Alonso, Angel Fernandez, and Emiliano Díez. 2015. Subjective Age-of-Acquisition norms for 7,039 Spanish Words. *Behavior Research Methods* 47(1):268–274.

Sandra M. Aluísio, Lucia Specia, Thiago A. S. Pardo, Erick G. Maziero, Helena M. Caseli, and Renata P. M. Fortes. 2008. A Corpus Analysis of Simple Account Texts and the Proposal of Simplification Strategies: First Steps Towards Text Simplification Systems. In *Proceedings of the 26th Annual ACM International Conference on Design of Communication*. ACM, SIGDOC '08, pages 15–22.

S.M. Aluísio and C. Gasperin. 2010. Fostering Digital Inclusion and Accessibility: The PorSimples Project for Simplification of Portuguese Texts. In *Proceedings of NAACL HLT 2010 YIWCALA*.

Ricardo A. Baeza-Yates, Luz Rello, and Julia Dembowski. 2015. CASSA: A Context-Aware Synonym Simplification Algorithm. In *NAACL HLT 2015*. pages 1380–1385.

Or Biran, Samuel Brody, and Noémie Elhadad. 2011. Putting It Simply: A Context-aware Approach to Lexical Simplification. In *Proceedings of the ACL 2011*. pages 496–501.

Stefan Bott, Luz Rello, Biljana Drndarevic, and Horacio Saggion. 2012. Can Spanish Be Simpler? LexSiS: Lexical Simplification for Spanish. In *Proceedings of COLING 2012*. pages 357–374.

Jan De Belder and Marie-Francine Moens. 2010. Text Simplification for Children. In *Proceedings of the SIGIR Workshop on Accessible Search Systems*. pages 19–26.

Siobhan Devlin and John Tait. 1998. The Use of a Psycholinguistic Database in the Simplification of Text for Aphasic Readers. In *Linguistic Databases*. pages 161–173.

Manaal Faruqui, Jesse Dodge, Sujay Kumar Jauhar, Chris Dyer, Eduard Hovy, and Noah A. Smith. 2015. Retrofitting Word Vectors to Semantic Lexicons. In *Proceedings of NAACL 2015*.

Daniel Ferrés, Ahmed AbuRa'ed, and Horacio Saggion. 2017. Spanish Morphological Generation with Wide-Coverage Lexicons and Decision Trees. *Procesamiento del Lenguaje Natural* 58:109–116.

Daniel Ferrés, Montserrat Marimon, Horacio Saggion, and Ahmed AbuRa'ed. 2016. YATS: Yet Another Text Simplifier. In *NLDB*. Springer, volume 9612 of *Lecture Notes in Computer Science*, pages 335–342.

Goran Glavaš and Sanja Štajner. 2015. Simplifying Lexical Simplification: Do We Need Simplified Corpora? In *Proceedings of ACL 2015*. pages 63–68.

Lluís Padró and Evgeny Stanilovsky. 2012. FreeLing 3.0: Towards Wider Multilinguality. In *Proceedings of LREC 2012*. ELRA.

Gustavo Paetzold and Lucia Specia. 2016. SemEval 2016 Task 11: Complex Word Identification. In *Proceedings of the 10th International Workshop on Semantic Evaluation*. pages 560–569.

Gustavo Henrique Paetzold. 2016. *Lexical Simplification for Non-Native English Speakers*. Ph.D. thesis, The University of Sheffield.

Sarah E. Petersen and Mari Ostendorf. 2007. Text Simplification for Language Learners: a Corpus Analysis. In *In Proc. of Workshop on Speech and Language Technology for Education*.

Horacio Saggion. 2017. *Automatic Text Simplification*. 32. Morgan & Claypool Publishers, 1 edition.

Horacio Saggion, Sanja Štajner, Stefan Bott, Simon Mille, Luz Rello, and Biljana Drndarevic. 2015. Making it Simplext: Implementation and Evaluation of a Text Simplification System for Spanish. *TACCESS* 6(4):14.

L. Specia, S. K. Jauhar, and R. Mihalcea. 2012. SemEval-2012 Task 1: English Lexical Simplification. In *Proceedings of *SEM 2012*.

Lucia Specia. 2010. Translating from Complex to Simplified Sentences. In *Proceedings of the 9th International Conference on Computational Processing of the Portuguese Language*. pages 30–39.

Sanja Stajner. 2014. Translating Sentences from Original to Simplified Spanish. *Procesamiento del lenguaje natural* 53:61–68.

P. D. Turney and P. Pantel. 2010. From Frequency to Meaning: Vector Space Models of Semantics. *J. Artif. Int. Res.* 37(1):141–188.

Krzysztof Wrobel. 2016. PLUJAGH at SemEval-2016 Task 11: Simple System for Complex Word Identification. In *Proceedings of the 10th International Workshop on Semantic Evaluation*. pages 953–957.

M. Yatskar, B. Pang, C. Danescu-Niculescu-Mizil, and L. Lee. 2010. For the Sake of Simplicity: Unsupervised Extraction of Lexical Simplifications from Wikipedia. In *Proceedings of HLT-NAACL 2010*.

Cross-genre Document Retrieval: Matching between Conversational and Formal Writings

Tomasz Jurczyk
Mathematics and Computer Science
Emory University
Atlanta, GA 30322, USA
tomasz.jurczyk@emory.edu

Jinho D. Choi
Mathematics and Computer Science
Emory University
Atlanta, GA 30322, USA
jinho.choi@emory.edu

Abstract

This paper challenges a cross-genre document retrieval task, where the queries are in formal writing and the target documents are in conversational writing. In this task, a query, is a sentence extracted from either a summary or a plot of an episode in a TV show, and the target document consists of transcripts from the corresponding episode. To establish a strong baseline, we employ the current state-of-the-art search engine to perform document retrieval on the dataset collected for this work. We then introduce a structure reranking approach to improve the initial ranking by utilizing syntactic and semantic structures generated by NLP tools. Our evaluation shows an improvement of more than 4% when the structure reranking is applied, which is very promising.

1 Introduction

Document retrieval has been a central task in natural language processing and information retrieval. The goal is to match a query against a set of documents. Over the last decade, advanced techniques have emerged and provided powerful systems that can accurately retrieve relevant documents (Blair and Maron, 1985; Callan, 1994; Cao et al., 2006). While the retrieval part is crucial, proper ranking of the retrieved documents can significantly improve the overall user satisfation by putting more relevant documents at the top (Baliński and Daniłowicz, 2005; Yang et al., 2006; Zhou and Wade, 2009). Many previous works provide strong baselines for unstructured text retrieval and ranking problems; however, these systems usually assume a homogeneous domain for queries and target documents.

Due to the spike of applications that are required to maintain the conversation, dialog data has recently become a popular target among researchers. The work in this field concerns problems such as learning facts through conversation (Fernández et al., 2011; Williams et al., 2015; Hixon et al., 2015) or dialog summarization (Oya and Carenini, 2014; Misra et al., 2015). More recent work in this field has focused on several inter-dialogue tasks (Xu and Reitter, 2016; Kim et al., 2016; He et al., 2016). To the best of our knowledge our work is the first, where the cross-genre document retrieval is analyzed based on conversational and formal writings.

This paper analyzes the performance of state-of-the-art retrieval techniques targeting TV show transcripts and their descriptions. We first collect a dataset comprising transcripts from a popular TV show and their summaries and plots (Section 3). We then establish a solid baseline by adapting an advanced search engine and implement structure reranking to improve the initial ranking from the search engine (Section 4). Our evaluation shows a 4% improvement, which is significant (Section 5).

2 Related work

Information extraction for dialogue data has already been widely explored. Yoshino et al. (2011) presented a spoken dialogue system that extracts predicate-argument structures and uses them to extract facts from news documents. Flycht-Eriksson and Jönsson (2003) developed a dialogue interaction process of accessing textual data from a bird encyclopedia. An unsupervised technique for meeting summarization using decision-related utterances has been presented by Wang and Cardie (2012). Gorinski and Lapata (2015) studied movie script summarization. All the aforementioned work uses the syntactic and semantic relation extraction and thus is similar to ours; however, it is distinguished in a way that it lacks a cross-genre aspect.

Proceedings of the First Workshop on Building Linguistically Generalizable NLP Systems, pages 48–53
Copenhagen, Denmark, September 8, 2017.

	Dialogue	Summary + Plot
Joey	One woman? That's like saying there's only one flavor of ice cream for you. Lemme tell you something, Ross. There's lots of flavors out there.	Joey compares women to ice cream. (*S*)
Ross Rachel	You know you probably didn't know this, but back in high school, I had a, um, major crush on you. I knew.	Ross reveals his high school crush on Rachel. (*S*)
Chandler Joey	Alright, one of you give me your underpants. Can't help you, I'm not wearing any.	Chandler asks Joey for his underwear, but Joey can't help him out as he's not wearing any. (*P*)

Table 1: Three manually curated examples of dialogues and their descriptions.

3 Data

The Character Mining project provides transcripts of the TV show, *Friends*; transcripts from 8 seasons of the show are publicly available in the JSON format,[1] where the first 2 seasons are annotated for the character identification task (Chen and Choi, 2016). Each season consists of episodes, each episode contains scenes, each scene includes utterances, where each utterance comes with the speaker information.

For each episode, the episode summary and plot are first collected from fan sites,[2] then sentence segmented by NLP4J,[3] the same tool used for the provided transcripts. Generally, summaries give broad descriptions of the episodes, whereas plots describe facts within individual scenes. Finally, we create a dataset by treating each sentence as a query and its relevant episode as the target document. Table 2 shows the distributions of this dataset.

Dialogue		Summary + Plot	
# of episodes	194	# of queries	5,075
# of tokens	897,446	# of tokens	119,624

Table 2: Dialogue, summary, and plot data.

4 Structure Reranking

For each query (summary or plot) in the dataset, the task is to retrieve the document (episode) most relevant to the query. The challenge comes from the cross-genre aspect: how to retrieve documents in dialogues given the queries in formal writing. This section describes our structure reranking approach that significantly outperforms an advanced search engine, Elasticsearch[4].

4.1 Relation Extraction

Since our queries and documents appear very different on the surface level (Table 1), relations are first extracted from them and matching is performed on the relation level, which abstracts certain pragmatic differences between these two types of writings. All data are lemmatized, tagged with parts-of-speech and named entities, parsed into dependency trees, and labeled with semantic roles using NLP4J.

A sentence may consist of multiple predicates, and each predicate comes with a set of arguments. A predicate together with its arguments is considered a relation. For each argument, heuristics are applied to extract meaningful contextual words by traversing the subtree of the argument. Our heuristics are designed for the type of dependency trees generated by NLP4J, but similar rules can be generalized to other types of dependency trees. Relations from dialogues are attached with the speaker names to compensate the lack of entity information.

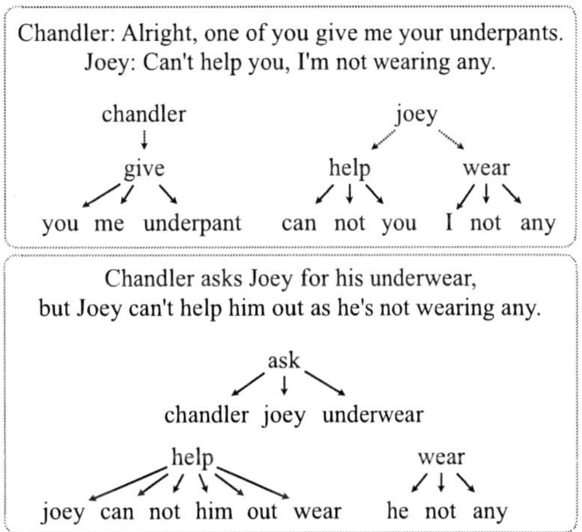

Figure 1: Two sets of relations, from dialogue and plot, extracted from the examples in Table 1.

By extracting relations that comprise only meaningful words, it prunes out much noise (e.g., disfluency), which allows the system to retrieve relevant documents with higher precision. While our relation extraction is based on the sentence level, it can be extended to the document level by adding coreference relations, which we will explore in the future.

[1] nlp.mathcs.emory.edu/character-mining
[2] friends-tv.org, friends.wikia.com
[3] github.com/emorynlp/nlp4j
[4] https://www.elastic.co/

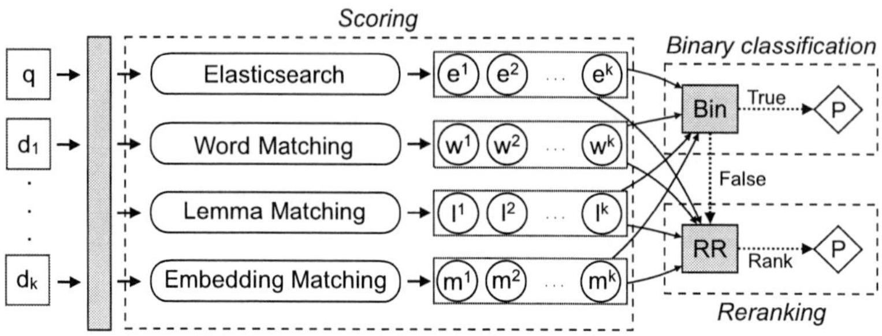

Figure 2: The overview of our structure reranking. Given documents $d_1, \ldots, d_k$ and a query q, 4 sets of scores are generated: the Elasticsearch scores and the matching scores using 3 comparators: *word*, *lemma*, and *embedding*. The binary classifier `Bin` predicts whether the highest ranked document from Elasticsearch is the correct answer. If not, the system `RR` reranks the documents using all scores and returns a new top-ranked prediction.

4.2 Structure Matching

All relations extracted from dialogues are stored in an inverted index manner, where words in each relation are associated with the relation and the episode in which the relation occurs. Algorithm 1 shows how our structure matching works. Given a list of documents retrieved from the index based on a query q, it first initializes scores for all documents to 0. For each document d_i, it compares each relation r^q from q to relations extracted from d_i. The relation r from d_i is kept within R^d if it has at least one word that overlaps with r^q. For each relation $r^d \in R^d$, the comparator function returns the matching score between r^d and r^q. The maximum matching score is added to the overall score of this document. This procedure is repeated; finally, the algorithm returns the overall matching scores for all documents.

```
Input: D: a list of documents, q: a query.
       f_r: a function returning all relations.
       f_c: a comparator function.
Output: S: a list of matching scores for D.
S ← [0 for i ∈ [1, |S|]
foreach d_i ∈ D do
    foreach r^q ∈ f_r(q) do
        R^d ← [r for r ∈ f_r(d_i) if |r ∩ r^q| ≥ 1]
        s_m ← 0
        foreach r^d in R^d do
            s ← f_c(r^d, r^q)
            s_m ← max(s_m, s)
        end
        S_i ← S_i + s_m
    end
end
```

Algorithm 1: The structure matching algorithm.

The comparator function f_c takes two relation sets, r^d and r^q, and returns the matching score between those two sets. For $word$ and $lemma$, the count of overlapping words between them is used to produce two scores, r^d_s, and r^q_s, normalized by the length of the utterance and the query, respectively. The harmonic mean of the two scores is then returned as the final score. For $embedding$, f_c uses embeddings to generate sum vectors from both sets and returns the cosine similarity of these two vectors.

4.3 Document Reranking

The Elasticsearch scores and the 3 sets of matching scores for the top-k documents (ranked by Elasticsearch) are fed into a binary classifier to determine whether or not to accept the highest ranked document. A Feed Forward Neural Network with one hidden layer of size 15 is used for this classification. If the binary classifier disqualifies the top-ranked document, the top-k documents are reranked by the weighted sums of these scores. A grid search is performed on the development set to find the optimized set of the weights. At last, the system returns the document with the highest reranked scores:
$d_i = \arg\max_i(\lambda_e \cdot e_i + \lambda_w \cdot w_i + \lambda_l \cdot l_i + \lambda_m \cdot m_i)$.

5 Experiments

The data in Section 3 is split into training, development and evaluation sets, where queries from each episode are randomly assigned. Two standard metrics are used for evaluation: precision at k (P@k) and mean reciprocal rank (MRR).

Dataset	Summary	Plot	Total
Training	970	3,013	3,983 (78.48%)
Development	97	403	500 (9.85%)
Evaluation	150	442	592 (11.67%)

Table 3: Data split (# of queries).

Model	Development						Evaluation					
	Summary		Plot		All		Summary		Plot		All	
	P@1	MRR	P@1	MRR	P@1	MRR	P@1	MRR	P@1	MRR	P@1	MRR
Elastic_{10}	44.33	53.64	46.40	54.97	46.00	54.71	50.67	60.87	46.61	55.06	47.64	56.53
Struct_w	38.14	48.42	34.00	45.11	34.80	45.75	35.33	48.34	35.52	47.08	35.47	47.40
Struct_l	39.18	49.24	34.74	46.29	**35.60**	**46.86**	44.00	55.55	38.01	49.24	**39.53**	**50.84**
Struct_m	35.05	46.71	33.50	44.72	33.80	45.10	36.00	50.14	35.97	46.95	35.98	47.76
Rerank_1	47.42	55.66	48.39	56.10	48.20	56.02	56.67	63.77	50.23	57.99	51.86	59.46
Rerank_λ	50.52	57.66	51.36	57.76	**51.20**	**57.74**	55.33	63.88	50.90	58.47	**52.03**	**59.84**

Table 4: Evaluation on the development and evaluation sets for summary, plot, and all (summary + plot). Elastic_{10}: Elasticsearch with $k = 10$, $\text{Struct}_{w,l,m}$: structure matching using words, lemmas, embeddings, $\text{Rerank}_{1,\lambda}$: unweighted and weighted reranking.

5.1 Elasticsearch

Elasticsearch is used to establish a strong baseline.[5] Each episode is indexed as a document using the default setting, Okapi BM25 (Robertson et al., 2009), and the TF-IDF based similarity with improved normalization; the top-k most relevant documents are retrieved for each query. While P@1 is less than 50% (Table 5), P@10 shows greater than 70% coverage implying that it is possible to achieve a higher P@1 by reranking results from $k \geq 10$.

k	Development		Evaluation	
	P@k	MRR	P@k	MRR
1	**46.00**	46.00	**47.64**	47.64
5	65.80	53.80	69.26	69.26
10	72.60	**54.71**	74.66	**56.53**
20	78.80	55.13	79.73	56.91
40	83.80	55.31	84.80	57.08

Table 5: Elasticsearch results on (summary + plot).

5.2 Structure Matching

The Struct_* rows in Table 4 show the results based on structure matching (Section 4.2). The highest P@1 of 39.53% is achieved on the evaluation set using lemmas. Although it is about 8% lower than the one achieved by Elasticsearch, we hypothesize that this approach can correctly retrieve documents for certain queries that Elasticsearch cannot.

Model	Development		Evaluation	
	P@1	MRR	P@1	MRR
Elastic_{10}	0	16.07	0	16.99
Struct_w	14.44	23.57	19.68	28.11
Struct_l	14.81	**25.59**	**20.97**	**30.14**
Struct_e	**15.56**	24.47	20.32	29.22

Table 6: Results on queries failed by Elasticsearch.

To validate our hypothesis, we test structure matching on the subset of queries failed by Elasticsearch. We first take the top-10 results from Elasticsearch then rerank the results using the scores from structure matching for queries that Elasticsearch gives P@1 of 0%. As shown in Table 6, structure matching is capable of reranking a significant portion (around 20%) of these queries correctly, establishing that our hypothesis is true.

5.3 Document Reranking

The scores from Elastic_{10} and Struct_* for each document are fed into the binary classifier that decides whether or not to accept the top-1 result from Elasticsearch. If not, the documents are reranked by the weighted sum of these scores (Section 4.3). The Rerank_1 row in Table 4 shows the results when all the weights = 1, which gives an over 4% improvement of P@1 on the evaluation set. The Rerank_λ row shows the results when the optimized weights are used, which gives an additional 3% boost on the development set but not on the evaluation set.

It is worth mentioning that we initially tackled this as a document classification task using convolutional neural networks similar to Kim (2014); however, it gave P@1 $\approx$ 20% and MRR $\approx$ 33%. Such poor results were due to the huge size of our documents, over 4.6K words on average, beyond the capacity of a CNN. Thus, we decided to focus on reranking, which gave the best performance.

6 Conclusion

We propose a cross-genre document retrieval task that matches between TV show transcripts and their descriptions in summaries and plots. Our structure reranking approach gives an improvement of more than 4% of P@1, showing promising results for this task. In the future, we will add more structural information such as coreference relations to our structure matching and apply a more sophisticated parameter optimization technique such as the Bayesian optimization for finding λ_*.

[5] www.elastic.co/products/elasticsearch

References

Jaroslaw Baliński and Czeslaw Daniłowicz. 2005. Reranking method based on inter-document distances. *Information processing & management* 41(4):759–775.

David C Blair and Melvin E Maron. 1985. An evaluation of retrieval effectiveness for a full-text document-retrieval system. *Communications of the ACM* 28(3):289–299.

James P Callan. 1994. Passage-level evidence in document retrieval. In *Proceedings of the 17th annual international ACM SIGIR conference on Research and development in information retrieval*. Springer-Verlag New York, Inc., pages 302–310.

Yunbo Cao, Jun Xu, Tie-Yan Liu, Hang Li, Yalou Huang, and Hsiao-Wuen Hon. 2006. Adapting ranking svm to document retrieval. In *Proceedings of the 29th annual international ACM SIGIR conference on Research and development in information retrieval*. ACM, pages 186–193.

Yu-Hsin Chen and Jinho D. Choi. 2016. Character identification on multiparty conversation: Identifying mentions of characters in tv shows. In *Proceedings of the 17th Annual Meeting of the Special Interest Group on Discourse and Dialogue*. Association for Computational Linguistics, Los Angeles, pages 90–100. http://www.aclweb.org/anthology/W16-3612.

Raquel Fernández, Staffan Larsson, Robin Cooper, Jonathan Ginzburg, and David Schlangen. 2011. Reciprocal learning via dialogue interaction: Challenges and prospects. In *Proceedings of the IJCAI 2011 Workshop on Agents Learning Interactively from Human Teachers (ALIHT 2011)*.

Annika Flycht-Eriksson and Arne Jönsson. 2003. Some empirical findings on dialogue management and domain ontologies in dialogue systems - implications from an evaluation of birdquest. In Akira Kurematsu, Alexander Rudnicky, and Syun Tutiya, editors, *Proceedings of the Fourth SIGdial Workshop on Discourse and Dialogue*. pages 158–167. http://www.aclweb.org/anthology/W03-2113.

Philip John Gorinski and Mirella Lapata. 2015. Movie script summarization as graph-based scene extraction. In *Proceedings of the 2015 Conference of the North American Chapter of the Association for Computational Linguistics: Human Language Technologies*. Association for Computational Linguistics, Denver, Colorado, pages 1066–1076. http://www.aclweb.org/anthology/N15-1113.

Zhiyang He, Xien Liu, Ping Lv, and Ji Wu. 2016. Hidden softmax sequence model for dialogue structure analysis. In *Proceedings of the 54th Annual Meeting of the Association for Computational Linguistics (Volume 1: Long Papers)*. Association for Computational Linguistics, Berlin, Germany, pages 2063–2072. http://www.aclweb.org/anthology/P16-1194.

Ben Hixon, Peter Clark, and Hannaneh Hajishirzi. 2015. Learning knowledge graphs for question answering through conversational dialog. In *HLT-NAACL*. pages 851–861.

Seokhwan Kim, Rafael Banchs, and Haizhou Li. 2016. Exploring convolutional and recurrent neural networks in sequential labelling for dialogue topic tracking. In *Proceedings of the 54th Annual Meeting of the Association for Computational Linguistics (Volume 1: Long Papers)*. Association for Computational Linguistics, Berlin, Germany, pages 963–973. http://www.aclweb.org/anthology/P16-1091.

Yoon Kim. 2014. Convolutional Neural Networks for Sentence Classification. In *Proceedings of the 2014 Conference on Empirical Methods in Natural Language Processing*. Association for Computational Linguistics, Doha, Qatar, EMNLP'14, pages 1746–1751. http://www.aclweb.org/anthology/D14-1181.

Amita Misra, Pranav Anand, Jean E. Fox Tree, and Marilyn Walker. 2015. Using summarization to discover argument facets in online idealogical dialog. In *Proceedings of the 2015 Conference of the North American Chapter of the Association for Computational Linguistics: Human Language Technologies*. Association for Computational Linguistics, Denver, Colorado, pages 430–440. http://www.aclweb.org/anthology/N15-1046.

Tatsuro Oya and Giuseppe Carenini. 2014. Extractive summarization and dialogue act modeling on email threads: An integrated probabilistic approach. In *Proceedings of the 15th Annual Meeting of the Special Interest Group on Discourse and Dialogue (SIGDIAL)*. Association for Computational Linguistics, Philadelphia, PA, U.S.A., pages 133–140. http://www.aclweb.org/anthology/W14-4318.

Stephen Robertson, Hugo Zaragoza, et al. 2009. The probabilistic relevance framework: Bm25 and beyond. *Foundations and Trends® in Information Retrieval* 3(4):333–389.

Lu Wang and Claire Cardie. 2012. Focused meeting summarization via unsupervised relation extraction. In *Proceedings of the 13th Annual Meeting of the Special Interest Group on Discourse and Dialogue*. Association for Computational Linguistics, Seoul, South Korea, pages 304–313. http://www.aclweb.org/anthology/W12-1642.

Jason D Williams, Nobal B Niraula, Pradeep Dasigi, Aparna Lakshmiratan, Carlos Garcia Jurado Suarez, Mouni Reddy, and Geoff Zweig. 2015. Rapidly scaling dialog systems with interactive learning. In *Natural Language Dialog Systems and Intelligent Assistants*, Springer, pages 1–13.

Yang Xu and David Reitter. 2016. Entropy converges between dialogue participants: Explanations from an information-theoretic perspective. In *Proceedings of the 54th Annual Meeting of the*

Association for Computational Linguistics (Volume 1: Long Papers). Association for Computational Linguistics, Berlin, Germany, pages 537–546. http://www.aclweb.org/anthology/P16-1051.

Lingpeng Yang, Donghong Ji, Guodong Zhou, Yu Nie, and Guozheng Xiao. 2006. Document re-ranking using cluster validation and label propagation. In *Proceedings of the 15th ACM international conference on Information and knowledge management*. ACM, pages 690–697.

Koichiro Yoshino, Shinsuke Mori, and Tatsuya Kawahara. 2011. Spoken dialogue system based on information extraction using similarity of predicate argument structures. In *Proceedings of the SIGDIAL 2011 Conference*. Association for Computational Linguistics, Portland, Oregon, pages 59–66. http://www.aclweb.org/anthology/W11-2008.

Dong Zhou and Vincent Wade. 2009. Latent document re-ranking. In *Proceedings of the 2009 Conference on Empirical Methods in Natural Language Processing: Volume 3-Volume 3*. Association for Computational Linguistics, pages 1571–1580.

ACTSA: Annotated Corpus for Telugu Sentiment Analysis

Sandeep Sricharan Mukku and **Radhika Mamidi**
Language Technologies Research Center
KCIS, IIIT Hyderabad
sandeep.mukku@research.iiit.ac.in, radhika.mamidi@iiit.ac.in

Abstract

Sentiment analysis deals with the task of determining the polarity of a document or sentence and has received a lot of attention in recent years for the English language. With the rapid growth of social media these days, a lot of data is available in regional languages besides English. Telugu is one such regional language with abundant data available in social media, but it's hard to find a labelled data of sentences for Telugu Sentiment Analysis. In this paper, we describe an effort to build a gold-standard annotated corpus of Telugu sentences to support Telugu Sentiment Analysis. The corpus, named ACTSA (Annotated Corpus for Telugu Sentiment Analysis) has a collection of Telugu sentences taken from different sources which were then preprocessed and manually annotated by native Telugu speakers using our annotation guidelines. In total, we have annotated 5410 sentences, which makes our corpus the largest resource currently available. The corpus and annotation guidelines are made publicly available.

1 Introduction

Now-a-days, people are commonly found writing comments, reviews, blog posts in social media about trending activities in their regional languages. Unlike English, many regional languages lack NLP tools and resources to analyze these activities. Moreover, English has many datasets available, however, it is not the same with Telugu.

The annotation of Telugu data has not received a lot of attention in sentiment analysis community. While there is a wealth of raw corpora with opinionated information, no corpora with annotated sentences in Telugu are publicly available as far as we know.

Telugu has a special status as an official standard language in the twin states of Andhra Pradesh and Telangana of India. There are a large variety of dialects that constitute the mother tongues of Telugu speakers. Major Telugu print media, journalism, and electronic media follow the dialects of Krishna and Godavari since it has been conceived as arguably standard and easy to reach the rest of the Telugu speakers (Krishnamurthi, 1961). We built our corpus over this dialect as this dialect is most prominent and has a strong online presence today on news websites, blogs, forums, and user/reader commentaries.

In this work, we present a dedicated gold standard corpus of polarity annotated Telugu sentences. To our knowledge, our corpus is the largest source of polarity annotated Telugu sentences to date. This data also motivates the development of new techniques for Telugu sentiment analysis. The corpus and annotation guidelines are publicly available here[1].

2 Related Work

There is a growing interest within the Natural Language Processing community to build corpora for Indian languages from the data available on the web. (Kaur and Gupta, 2013) surveyed sentiment analysis for different Indian languages including Telugu, but never mentioned about the corpus used. (Mukku et al., 2016) did sentiment classification for Telugu

[1] https://goo.gl/M9rkUX

Proceedings of the First Workshop on Building Linguistically Generalizable NLP Systems, pages 54–58
Copenhagen, Denmark, September 8, 2017.

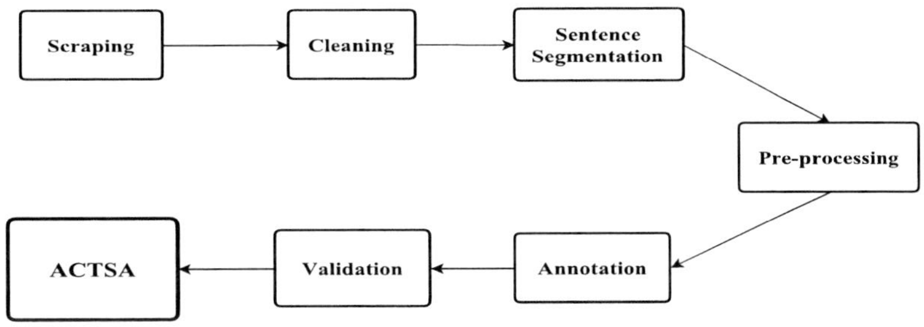

Figure 1: Process of building the resource

text using various ML techniques, but no data was publicly made available.

(Wiebe et al., 2005) describes a corpus annotation project to study issues in the manual annotation of opinions, emotions, sentiments, speculations, evaluations and other private states in language. This was the first attempt to manually annotate the 10,000 sentence corpus of articles from the news. (Alm et al., 2005) have manually annotated 1580 sentences extracted from 22 Grimms' tales for the task of emotion annotation at the sentence level.

(Arora, 2013) performed sentiment analysis task for the Hindi Language with limited corpus made manually annotated by the native Hindi speakers. (Das and Bandyopadhyay, 2010b) aims to manually annotate the sentences in a web-based Bengali blog corpus with the emotional components such as emotional expression (word/phrase), intensity, associated holder and topic(s).

(Das and Bandyopadhyay, 2010a) built a lexicon of words to support the task of Telugu sentiment analysis and is made available to the public. (Das and Bandyopadhay, 2010) created an interactive gaming to technology (Dr. Sentiment) to create and validate SentiWordNet for Telugu.

3 Data Collection

In this section, we will explore the different resources where raw data was obtained from and how processing of that data was done, as shown in Figure 1.

Currently, most of the corpora available for Sentiment Analysis are harvested from sources like review data from e-commerce websites where customers express their opinion on products freely, posts from social networking sites like Twitter and Facebook. Although the news genre has received much less attention within the Sentiment Analysis community, news plays an important role in exhibiting the reality and has a strong influence on social practices. Also, a lot of Telugu data is available mostly on news websites. These reasons motivated us to select news genre for building our corpus. We scraped and harvested our raw data from five different Telugu news websites viz., Andhrabhoomi[2], Andhrajyothi[3], Eenadu[4], Kridajyothi[5] and Sakshi[6]. In total we have collected over 453 news articles and filtered down to 321 which were relevant to our work.

The extracted data was cleaned in a preprocessing step, e.g. by removing headings and sub-headings, eliminating sentences with non-Telugu words and cleaning any extra dots, extra spaces, URLs, and other garbage values. Later *Sentence Segmentation* is done where this data was split into individual sentences.

The sentences thus obtained were now tested for objectivity manually. Objective sentences are sentences where no sentiment, opinion, etc. is expressed. They state a fact confidently and has an evidence to support it. For example, sentence (1) is an objective sentence as it is a verifiable fact with evidence.

అబ్దుల్ కలాం భారతదేశ అధ్యక్షుడిగా పనిచేశారు (1)

Transliteration: Abdul kalāṁ bhāratadēśa adhyakṣuḍigā panicēśāru
English: Abdul Kalam served as the president of India

[2] http://www.andhrabhoomi.net/
[3] http://www.andhrajyothy.com/
[4] http://www.eenadu.net/
[5] http://www.andhrajyothy.com/pages/sports
[6] http://www.sakshi.com/

Table 1: Example annotations

ID	Original Sentence	English Translation	A1	A2	V	F
1	అమెరికా అధ్యక్షుడు డోనాల్డ్ ట్రంప్ పారిస్ వాతావరణ ఒప్పందం నుంచి అమెరికాను వైదొలగించారు	US President Donald Trump withdrew the US from the Paris Climate Agreement	Neg	Obj	Obj	Obj
2	ఇందుకు ఎవరికీ అభ్యంతరం ఉండనవసరం లేదు	There is no need for any objection to anyone in this	Neu	Neu	NA	Neu
3	భారత ప్రధానమంత్రి నరేంద్రమోడీ కాశ్మీర్ అల్లర్లపై ఘాటుగా స్పందించారు	India's Prime Minister Narendra Modi has reacted severely to the Kashmir riots	Neg	Neg	NA	Neg
4	ఫలితాలపై మంత్రి సంతోషంగా ఉన్నారు	The minister is happy on the results	Pos	Pos	NA	Pos

Pos = Positive, Neg = Negative, Neu = Neutral, Obj = Objective, NA = Not Applicable, A1 = Annotator 1, A2 = Annotator 2, V = Validation, F = Final Result

These sentences do not contain any sentiment/polarity and are not useful for sentiment analysis. The objective sentences thus separated with objectivity test are removed from the data.

4 Annotation

In this section, we describe the process followed for annotating the sentences (refer Figure 1). First, we built a team of seven educated native Telugu speakers for the task of polarity tagging of the extracted Telugu sentences. Then, we developed an annotation schema for this task and the annotators were instructed to thoroughly understand the concepts mentioned in the schema for a precise/perfect annotation. Each sentence is annotated by two annotators.

The annotators were required to tag the sentences with three polarities: *positive, negative, neutral.* For example, sentence (2) should be tagged *positive* as it expresses positive sentiment by the use of కృతజ్ఞత (gratitude).

మంత్రి, ఆయనను ఎన్నుకున్నందుకు, (2)

ప్రజలకు కృతజ్ఞత వ్యక్తం చేశారు
Transliteration: Mantri, āyananu ennukunnanduku, prajalaku krtajñata vyaktaṁ cēśāru
English: The minister expressed gratitude to the people for electing him

On the other hand sentence (3) should be tagged *negative* because it expresses negative sentiment with ఆందోళన (concern).

నిరంతర విద్యుత్ కోతలపై ప్రజలు ఆందోళన వ్యక్తం చేశారు (3)

Transliteration: Nirantara vidyut kōtalapai prajalu āndōḷana vyaktaṁ cēśāru
English: People have expressed concern over continuous power cuts

However, sentence (4) is a *neutral* sentence as it is a speculation about the future. Even though it doesn't contain any sentiment, it is not an objective sentence because it is not a verifiable fact or not something which happened in the past. It is speculating something to happen in the future.

ప్రధాని వచ్చే నెలలో చైనాను సందర్శించనున్నారు (4)

Transliteration: Pradhāni vaccē nelalō caināanu sandarśiñcanunnāru
English: The prime minister is expected to visit China next month

If in any case annotators were unsure or felt ambiguous about the polarity of a sentence they can label it *uncertain.* If they feel the sentence is objective but was not removed in

Table 2: Agreement for Sentences in ACTSA

Annotator 1 \ Annotator 2	Positive	Negative	Neutral	Total
Positive	1463	31	103	1597
Negative	23	1421	116	1560
Neutral	112	127	2427	2666
Total	1598	1579	2646	5823

the pre-processing step, they can mark it *objective*.

Annotators labelled all the sentences, with each sentence annotated by exactly two annotators. We call it *annotation* step. The sentences marked *uncertain* by at least one annotator were discarded to avoid any ambiguous sentences in the corpus.

The sentences which had a clash between the two annotators' labels were sent for a *third independent annotation* which we call as a *validation* step. The most common label among the three annotators was considered as the final label for the sentence. If even after the third annotation the disagreement prevailed, such sentences were discarded as we considered them too ambiguous for getting three different labels by three different annotators. If there were any objective sentences after the *validation* step, they were discarded.

Table 1 shows some example annotations from the corpus.

5 Agreement Study

After annotation task, we measured how reliable our annotation scheme was. To measure the reliability of our polarity annotation scheme, we conducted an inter-annotator agreement study on the annotated sentences. Table 2 shows the agreement for the two annotators' judgments for each sentence. We used Cohens´ kappa, κ which is calculated using formula (5)

$$\kappa = \frac{p_o - p_e}{1 - p_e} \quad (5)$$

where p_o is the relative observed agreement and p_e is the agreement by chance. In general, κ values between 0.6 and 0.8 are considered a substantial agreement. To our surprise we got the κ value to be 0.87, which is in perfect agreement and is an indication of the reliability of the annotations.

Table 3: Statistics about the data

News articles	321
Cleaned Sentences	11952
Objective Sentences (Removed)	4327
Uncertain Sentences (Removed)	1802
Disagreement Sentences	512
Classified	99
Removed	413
Positive sentences	1489
Negative sentences	1441
Neutral sentences	2475
Total sentences	5410

6 Corpus Statistics

In this section, we present the statistics about our data from raw data collection to final sentences. We scraped several websites for the data. We collected 453 news articles and filtered down to 321 which were relevant for our work. After pre-processing this raw data, we have 11952 sentences. We tested the sentences for subjectivity (as explained in section 3) and removed 4327 objective sentences after which we were left with 7812 sentences. These sentences were given to the annotators for the annotation as mentioned in section 4. 1802 sentences were removed where at least one annotator marked it *uncertain*. In the remaining 5823 sentences, 512 were with disagreement and were sent for third independent annotation. After the third annotation, 413 sentences were discarded if the disagreement prevailed or if they are objective. The final 5410 sentences forms the required annotated corpus, ACTSA. Statistics about our complete corpus can be found in Table 3.

7 Experiments and Evaluation

A strategy that can give very useful hints about the reliability of the annotated data is the comparison between the results of automated classification and human annotation.

(Mukku et al., 2016) described a method to perform automated classification of Telugu sentences into polarity tags: positive, negative and neutral. We followed this method to evaluate our data. We used 2000 sentences from our human automated corpus to train the model for automated classification.

To test the reliability of our annotated data, we compared the classification expressed by humans and that of the automated classifier trained above. The testing was done on the remaining 3410 sentences and the error rate was observed to be **12.3%** which hints the quality and reliability of the annotated corpus, ACTSA.

8 Conclusion

In this work, we presented a gold standard corpus of Telugu sentences taken from different resources, which were then cleaned and annotated by native Telugu speakers. For each sentence, we have a polarity label attached with it. We described our annotation process and gave an overview of our annotation schema. The results from our evaluation study show that our corpus has a reasonable inter-annotator agreement. The corpus and guidelines are publicly available. In future, we try to automate the task of annotation for new sentences with the help of ACTSA. We would also like to perform sentiment analysis task for Telugu, using this corpus.

Acknowledgements

We would like to thank all the members of annotation group (native Telugu speakers) for their tireless effort in this process. The work reported in this paper was supported by Kohli Center on Intelligent Systems.

References

Cecilia Ovesdotter Alm, Dan Roth, and Richard Sproat. 2005. Emotions from text: machine learning for text-based emotion prediction. In *Proceedings of the conference on human language technology and empirical methods in natural language processing*. Association for Computational Linguistics, pages 579–586.

Piyush Arora. 2013. Sentiment analysis for hindi language. *MS by Research in Computer Science, IIIT Hyderabad* .

Amitava Das and S Bandyopadhay. 2010. Dr sentiment creates sentiwordnet (s) for indian languages involving internet population. In *Proceedings of Indo-wordnet workshop*.

Amitava Das and Sivaji Bandyopadhyay. 2010a. Sentiwordnet for indian languages. *Asian Federation for Natural Language Processing, China* pages 56–63.

Dipankar Das and Sivaji Bandyopadhyay. 2010b. Labeling emotion in bengali blog corpus–a fine grained tagging at sentence level. In *Proceedings of the 8th Workshop on Asian Language Resources*. page 47.

Amandeep Kaur and Vishal Gupta. 2013. A survey on sentiment analysis and opinion mining techniques. *Journal of Emerging Technologies in Web Intelligence* 5(4):367–371.

Bh Krishnamurthi. 1961. Telugu verbal bases: A comparative and descriptive study.

Sandeep Sricharan Mukku, Nurendra Choudhary, and Radhika Mamidi. 2016. Enhanced sentiment classification of telugu text using ml techniques. In *4th Workshop on Sentiment Analysis where AI meets Psychology, 25th International Joint Conference on Artificial Intelligence*. page 29.

Janyce Wiebe, Theresa Wilson, and Claire Cardie. 2005. Annotating expressions of opinions and emotions in language. *Language resources and evaluation* 39(2):165–210.

Strawman: an Ensemble of Deep Bag-of-Ngrams for Sentiment Analysis

Kyunghyun Cho
Courant Institute & Center for Data Science,
New York University
kyunghyun.cho@nyu.edu

Abstract

This paper describes a builder entry, named "strawman", to the sentence-level sentiment analysis task of the "Build It, Break It" shared task of the First Workshop on Building Linguistically Generalizable NLP Systems. The goal of a builder is to provide an automated sentiment analyzer that would serve as a target for breakers whose goal is to find pairs of minimally-differing sentences that break the analyzer.

1 Data and Preprocessing

Data The organizers of the shared task provided two distinct types of training sets. The first set consists of usual sentences paired with their corresponding sentiment labels (+1 for positive and -1 for negative) and confidences (a real value between 0 and 1.) The other set consists of phrases paired similarly with sentiment labels and confidences. In the latter case, the sentiment label may be either -1, 1 or 0 which indicates neutral. There are 6920 sentences and 166,737 phrases.

As the goal of "strawman" is to build the most naive and straightforward baseline for the shared task, I have decided to use all the examples from both of the training sets whose sentiment labels were either -1 or 1. In other words, any phrase labelled neutral was discarded. The confidence scores were discarded as well.

The combined data was shuffled first, and then the first 160k examples were used for training and the last 10k examples for validation. I have decided to ignore 3,657 examples in-between.

Vocabulary The training dataset was lowercased in order to avoid an issue of data sparsity, as the size of the dataset is relatively small. Since the provided training examples were already tokenized to a certain degree, I have not attempted any further tokenization, other than removing a quotation mark """. In the case of blind development and test sets, I used spaCy[1] for automatic tokenization. At this stage, a vocabulary was built using all the n-gram's with n up to 2 from the entire training set. This resulted in a vocabulary of 102,608 unique n-gram's, and among them, I decided to use only the 100k most frequent n-grams.

2 Model and Training

The "strawman" is an ensemble of five deep bag-of-ngrams classifiers. Each classifier is a multi-layer perceptron consisting of an embedding layer which transforms one-hot vector representations of words into continuous vectors, averaging pooling, a 32-dim $\tanh$ hidden layer and a binary softmax layer. The classifier is trained to minimize cross-entropy loss using Adam (Kingma and Ba, 2014) with the default parameters. Each training run was early-stopped based on the validation accuracy and took approximately 10-20 minutes on the author's laptop which has a 2.2 GHz Intel Core i7 (8 cores) and does not have any GPU compute capability. The output distributions of all the five classifiers, which were initialized using distinct random seeds, were averaged to form an ensemble. The entire code was written in Python using PyTorch.[2] The implementation is publicly available at https://github.com/kyunghyuncho/strawman.

3 Result and Thoughts

Despite its simplicity and computational efficiency, the "strawman" fared reasonably well. The "strawman" was ranked first in terms of the aver-

[1] https://spacy.io/
[2] http://pytorch.org/

Proceedings of the First Workshop on Building Linguistically Generalizable NLP Systems, pages 59–60
Copenhagen, Denmark, September 8, 2017.

age F1 score on all the breakers' test cases, outperforming more sophisticated systems based on a recursive deep network (Builder Team 5, (Socher et al., 2013)) as well as a convolutional network (Builder Team 6, (Kalchbrenner et al., 2014)). When measured by the proportion of the test cases on which the system was broken (i.e., the system is correct only for one of the minimally difference sentences and wrong for the other), the "strawman" was ranked fourth out of six submissions, although the margin between the "strawman" and the best ranking system (Builder Team 2) was only about 1% out of 25.43% broken case rate, corresponding to 6 cases.

Although we must wait until the breakers' reports in order to understand better how those broken cases were generated, there are a few clear holes in the proposed "strawman". First, if any word is replaced so that a new bigram disappears from the predefined vocabulary of n-grams, the "strawman" could easily be thrown off. This could be addressed by character-level modelling (Ling et al., 2015; Kim et al., 2015) or a hybrid model (Miyamoto and Cho, 2016). Second, the "strawman" will be easily fooled by any non-compositional expression that spans more than two words. This is inevitable, as any expression longer than two words could only be viewed as a composition of multiple uni- and bi-grams. Third, the obvious pitfall of the "strawman" is that it was trained solely on the provided training set consisting of less than 7k full sentences. The "strawman" would only generalize up to a certain degree to any expression not present in the training set.

Acknowledgments

The author thanks support by eBay, TenCent, Facebook, Google and NVIDIA.

References

Nal Kalchbrenner, Edward Grefenstette, and Phil Blunsom. 2014. A convolutional neural network for modelling sentences. *arXiv preprint arXiv:1404.2188* .

Yoon Kim, Yacine Jernite, David Sontag, and Alexander M Rush. 2015. Character-aware neural language models. In *AAAI 2016*.

Diederik Kingma and Jimmy Ba. 2014. Adam: A method for stochastic optimization. *arXiv preprint arXiv:1412.6980* .

Wang Ling, Tiago Luís, Luís Marujo, Ramón Fernandez Astudillo, Silvio Amir, Chris Dyer, Alan W Black, and Isabel Trancoso. 2015. Finding function in form: Compositional character models for open vocabulary word representation. *arXiv preprint arXiv:1508.02096* .

Yasumasa Miyamoto and Kyunghyun Cho. 2016. Gated word-character recurrent language model. In *EMNLP*.

Richard Socher, Alex Perelygin, Jean Y Wu, Jason Chuang, Christopher D Manning, Andrew Y Ng, Christopher Potts, et al. 2013. Recursive deep models for semantic compositionality over a sentiment treebank. In *Proceedings of the conference on empirical methods in natural language processing (EMNLP)*. volume 1631, page 1642.

Breaking Sentiment Analysis of Movie Reviews

Ieva Staliūnaitė and **Ben Bonfil**
Utrecht University
i.r.staliunaite@students.uu.nl

Abstract

The current paper covers several strategies we used to 'break' predictions of sentiment analysis systems participating in the BLGNLP2017 workshop. Specifically, we identify difficulties of participating systems in understanding modals, subjective judgments, world-knowledge based references and certain differences in syntax and perspective.

1 Introduction

Participants in the BLGNLP2017 shared task were invited to either build sentiment analysis systems (as a *Builder* team) or break them, by compiling linguistically motivated test cases that result in false predictions (as a *Breaker* team). A data set of movie reviews was provided as the domain for participating systems and as a source for generating breaking test cases. As a Breaker team, our goal was to construct minimal pairs consisting of a review from the source data set, and a modified version of the review that would be used to evaluate the robustness or sensitivity of the participating systems predictions. The modified version of each review could either preserve the sentiment of the original review, or reverse it.

Movie reviews from *Rotten Tomatoes* are a good source for comments full of sentiment, as the informal setting provides for humor, pathos, wild comparisons, sarcasm, artistic expressions and the like. Hence, it was probably not an easy task for the Builder systems to analyze sentiments to begin with, and we tried to make it even harder. Based on the sentiment analysis of our linguistic examples it seems like there are several ways to trick the Builder systems.

In our own judgments of the provided items, we followed a positive/negative sentiment dichotomy, which was not always straightforward given the complexity of the data. However, even if a neutral sentiment option was included (as found in the predictions of some of the Builder system) it would not have accounted for the whole variation, as some items could have multiple plausible interpretations, affecting their perceived valence. Thus, it is important to bear in mind that the judgments provided by us might not always coincide with those of other people.

We begin this paper by describing the general rationale we had employed in creating our test cases. We then present some examples of sentences that broke the Builder systems and discuss the nature of the errors, and the main difficulties in analyzing sentiment. In addition, we discuss the linguistic processes that take place in inferring sentiment from the various examples.

2 Breaking Strategy

Our approach to judging sentiment was based on two implicit questions: "Would I watch this movie based on the comment?" and "Would the comment be likely accompanied by a five star evaluation?" Thus, our judgment relied on reviewers' description of enjoyment and quality as measurements of sentiment. In making the minimal pairs we employed a number of different strategies. We used our intuitions and knowledge of syntax, semantics and pragmatics in order to make big differences in meaning with superficially small changes. We tried to make realistic examples of movie evaluations, focusing on linguistic inferences that a machine might not be able to do.

When it comes to breaking predictions, the largest number of errors appeared with examples involving words that bear judgment, but are not inherently positive or negative on their own. We used modals and opinion adverbs to contribute to

Proceedings of the First Workshop on Building Linguistically Generalizable NLP Systems, pages 61–64
Copenhagen, Denmark, September 8, 2017.

the meaning of a phrase by providing information about the speaker's subjective stance. For instance, adverbs such as 'too', 'enough', 'hardly', 'supposedly', 'barely', 'seldom', 'rarely' and 'finally' all convey a relative stance in certain contexts. The use of such expressions changes the construal of the sentence so that the perspective of the subject of consciousness is foregrounded (Verhagen et al., 2007). Therefore, including such an adverb can change the valence of the sentence, such as in examples (1) and (2) below. While the truth-conditions of (2) would not change if 'hardly' was substituted with 'a little', the judgment of the speaker would disappear. Hence, the sentiment in this example is expressed by foregrounding the speaker's evaluation of the extent of the difference between the two types of movies. While most Builder systems classified (1) as positive, just about half of them classified (2) as negative:

(1) Munich is more measured and classy than Spielberg's action-adventures.

(2) Munich is hardly more measured and classy than Spielberg's action-adventures.

The examples above point to another tactic found in our test items. Namely, besides the valence that the adverb contributes in these examples, world-knowledge is also necessary to properly infer the speaker's meaning. Since the sentence uses a proper noun and refers to a well-known figure, it can bear great influence on the valence of the sentence as a whole. We used this strategy in making minimal pairs that proved to confuse the participating systems. It has been claimed in the literature that proper nouns are mostly used in objective or neutral sentences (Pak and Paroubek, 2010). However, proper nouns can also carry sentiments in certain contexts. For instance, while Shakespearean is always a compliment, E.L. James-ian might not be. Most systems categorized (3) as positive, however a few of them missed the negative connotations of (4).

(3) Shakespearean in its violence, Oldboy also calls up nightmare images of spiritual and physical isolation that are worthy of Samuel Beckett or Dostoyevsky.

(4) EL James-ian in its violence, Oldboy also calls up nightmare images of spiritual and physical isolation that are worthy of Paulo Coelho quotes.

We think that world-knowledge could be included in the sentiment analysis systems and it would benefit the judgment of examples such as the one above. Even though this might appear as a non-linguistic issue, references and comparisons with well known directors or actors are found in many of the original reviews and play a role in determining the sentiment.

We have identified another difficulty in pragmatics that is prominent in movie reviews. In examples (5) and (6) below, the mention of the reader's expectations can mean very different things depending on the context:

(5) Sharp dialogue and detailed observations make it a good deal funnier than you might expect.

(6) Horrible dialogue and abysmal acting make it a good deal funnier than you might expect.

The minimal pair of (5) and (6) sheds light on the issue of whether calling a movie funny is a positive comment. This brings us to the discussion of the multi-layered sentiment structure. That is, while 'funny' refers to a positive emotion experienced by someone watching the movie, that might not be a positive comment on the movie, if it is the poor quality of acting that causes one to laugh, such as in example (6). We constructed a similar example where 'emotional pain' was experienced when watching the movie, which could be used to either admire or ridicule the movie. These examples show that the meaning of positive or negative adjectives can change with varying circumstances, such as expectations.

Furthermore, we used another strategy that is based on expressing expectations. A concessive relation, as found in (7) and (8), expresses a contrast between two statements. One of the statements in each sentence is positive and the other one is negative, however the overall sentiment of the two sentences differs. This is achieved by the fact that concessive relations have an expectation in the first component and deny that expectation in the second (Izutsu, 2008). This denial of expectation puts argumentative emphasis on the second part of the sentence, making the second judgment of the sentence stronger. This is why (7) is negative, while (8) is positive. However, many of the Builder systems had difficulty categorizing both sentences, as they include both positive and negative statements.

(7) It's harmless, sure, but it's also charmless.

(8) It's not harmless, sure, but it's also not charmless.

Another factor we found to affect the valence of the whole sentence, is the use of positive or negative adjectives to refer to a character in the movie or to the plot, but not to the movie itself. For example, the 'smoldering, humorless intensity' in (9) and (10) is a negative attribute of a person, but it might make a great character, such as in (10). However, a few of the Builder systems did not recognize it as a positive review.

(9) [Bettis] has a smoldering, humorless intensity that's unnerving.

(10) [Bettis] has a smoldering, humorless intensity that's hilarious.

As can be seen from the example above, treating words as separate entities with emotional valence can sometimes fail in analyzing sentiment of complete sentences. This leads to another strategy, which is changing the structure of the sentence with minimal changes in the lexical items used. For example, the sentences in (11) and (12) differ minimally in terms of the words used, but they have completely different syntactic structures. The syntactic dependencies determine what is the subject of the sentence and thus who is the savior and who we are saved from.

(11) Someone has to save us from Lawrence's onslaught of cinematic dross.

(12) Lawrence is someone who has saved us from an onslaught of cinematic dross.

Furthermore, syntactic structures can also introduce implicatures. For instance, we changed a sentence into a question or added a tag question and it resulted in Builder system errors. It can be seen from examples (13) and (14) that the sentences are nearly the same, except one of them is declarative and the second one is interrogative. Especially in combination with the use of ellipsis, sentence (14) implies doubt by the speaker, since they are asking a rhetorical question, provided the context is a movie review. Even though there is no explicit negation, the speaker explicitly does not commit to a positive statement. Implicatures are derived from the fact that the speaker did not use a more informative or stronger expression when they could have (Potts, 2015). In this case, if the speaker had found the movie exceptional, they would have said so. Many Builder systems did not recognize it as carrying negative sentiment.

(13) An exceptional science fiction film...

(14) Is this an exceptional science fiction film...?

We also employed ellipsis to change perspective and imply different content in the omitted part. In elliptical sentences, a part of the syntactic structure is missing, as demonstrated in examples (15) and (16) (the part in brackets was omitted in the items). The addition of 'please' to sentence (16) changes it from a declarative sentence to an imperative one. Elliptical utterances are reduced, therefore knowing the discourse goal of the speaker would facilitate the interpretation of the utterance (Carberry, 1989). Hence, the difference between sentences (15) and (16) can be inferred from the fact that one is a claim and the other is a request. Many of the Builder systems did not perform well on sentence (16).

(15) [This is] more of the same...

(16) [I want/give me] more of the same, please!

In addition, a couple of hypothetical sentences with implied content also confused the Builder systems. For example, the difference between (17) and (18) is simply the mood of the verb. The hypothetical in (18) implies that in fact the movie is not a good adaptation, as reality is different from what could have been. In other items, we used the verb 'to try' for an analogous effect, as claiming that someone tried to achieve something, implies that they did not succeed. In both cases almost all of the systems predicted the direct statement correctly, but did not register the implicature.

(17) Pride and Prejudice is a gorgeous and well-acted adaptation.

(18) Pride and Prejudice could have been a gorgeous and well-acted adaptation.

A final strategy that we adopted in developing our examples is the use of special characters and punctuation marks to affect meaning. In example (19), we used an explicit 'A+' grade, which frames the comment as positive feedback, even if it is preceded by a proposition that is negative on its own.

(19) Ridiculous, confusing, vaguely noir-ish nonsense. A+

All Builder systems failed to recognize it as a good movie mark, probably because such characters are filtered from input. Similarly, the quotation marks in (21) embed the speaker's statement as said by someone else, which in turn, together with an opposing comment, contests the original negative review. This was also not caught by the Builder systems. The change of subject of consciousness or speaker could even be done without the quotation marks, as the very contradictory statements could not both be held by one person, and the second phrase in (21) is clearly a retort.

(20) Flawed, clich, contrived, and poorly developed...

(21) "Flawed, clich, contrived, and poorly developed..." What do they know.

3 Conclusion

To conclude, we have shown how the rich and informal domain of movie reviews allows for sentences that are difficult to analyze for valence. Further manipulation had succeeded in creating items that are not properly understood by the participating systems. In particular, our results suggest that the context of a movie review allows for pragmatic and stylistic manipulations that pose difficulties to current systems. The identification of some of those difficulties might contribute to the improvement of sentiment analysis systems.

References

Sandra Carberry. 1989. A pragmatics-based approach to ellipsis resolution. *Computational Linguistics*, 15(2):75–96.

Mitsuko Narita Izutsu. 2008. Contrast, concessive, and corrective: Toward a comprehensive study of opposition relations. *Journal of Pragmatics*, 40(4):646–675.

Alexander Pak and Patrick Paroubek. 2010. Twitter as a corpus for sentiment analysis and opinion mining. In *LREc*, volume 10.

Christopher Potts. 2015. Presupposition and implicature. *The handbook of contemporary semantic theory*, 2:168–202.

Arie Verhagen et al. 2007. Construal and perspectivisation.

Author Index

Association for Computational Linguistics
209 N. Eighth Street
Stroudsburg, Pennsylvania 18360

ISBN 978-1-5108-4747-7

CURRAN ASSOCIATES INC.
proceedings.com